Here is the story of a cycling club which began in a suburban corner of Kent in the early 1970s and faded away 20 years later. May the Wheel of Fortune bring back Green Street Green Cycling Club – nosh-and-natter evenings and all!

Founded by a very special man – with his own language and a penchant for disused railway lines and instant mashed potato – at its peak the club had well over 500 members. But this is far more than a nostalgic look back at a defunct cycling club written by an old member, for old members. It is a quietly hilarious look at an eccentric slice of English life – a chronicle that draws in the outsider with its very English humour, everyday observations and delightfully amateurish illustrations. Anyone who has ever cycled, been a member of a club or lived in the suburbs will identify with this story of triumphs, disappointments and might-have-beens. Others can regret what they have missed.

Philip Turner was born in Chelsfield in Kent. After attending Ravenswood School in Bromley, he went on to graduate from Norwich UEA in 1983. He was an active member of the Green Street Green Cycling Club in 1977 and 1978 and, sporadically, between 1980–88. A vehicle inspector and writer, Philip is the author of *Caution! Used Cars: The Definitive Guide to Buying Secondhand Cars,* and *Buying Your Next Car: Your Questions Answered.* He has also contributed articles to *AutoExpress, Buying Cars/Car Choice, Jalopy* and *Kent Today* publications.

Also by Philip Turner:

Caution! Used Cars: A Step by Step Guide to Buying a Better Used Car and Selling the One You Own (SPA, 1991)

Caution! Used Cars: The Definitive Guide to Buying Secondhand Cars (Penguin, 1994)

Buying Your Next Car: Your Questions Answered (Otter, 1996)

THE STORY OF THE GREEN STREET GREEN CYCLING CLUB

Philip D. Turner

The Book Guild Ltd
Sussex, England

Any real-life resemblance to any of the people named below is entirely intentional. It must be remembered however that for the most part the events described in the text occurred perhaps as long as 20 years ago, and there has had to be an extensive reliance on memories of when most of us were little more than schoolchildren. In any case, the authors would wish to point out that it has not been their intention to hurt or offend in any way while recounting the story of the Green Street Green Cycling Club years.

This book is sold subject to the condition that it shall not, by way of trade or otherwise, be lent, re-sold, hired out, photocopied or held in any retrieval system or otherwise circulated without the publisher's prior consent in any form of binding or cover other than that in which this is published and without a similar condition including this condition being imposed on the subsequent purchaser.

The Book Guild Ltd.
25 High Street,
Lewes, Sussex

First published 1996
© Philip D. Turner 1996
Set in Times

Typesetting by Acorn Bookwork, Salisbury

Printed in Great Britain by
Bookcraft (Bath) Ltd, Avon

A catalogue record for this book is available from the British Library

ISBN 1 85776 116 2

In memory of former club members Danny Wilkinson (No. 7) and Glenn Huckfield (No. 17), sadly no longer with us

CONTENTS

List of Figures	x
Foreword by Ken Bird	xiii
Acknowledgements	xiv
Introduction	xv

1   The Club's Founder   1
The Early Rides, 1972–74 – Key Personnel, 1972–74

2   Up and Running and Gathering Speed   9
Longer Trips, Farther Afield, 1974–75 – The Green Street Green Cycling Club 'Official' Club Room

3   A Cycling Club Proper, 1975–76   11
Introduction to Time-Trialling and Cyclo-Cross – Sponsored Rides, Club Badges and T-Shirts, and the Forming of the Committee – A Sponsored Ride for Club Badges – 'Time, Gentlemen, Please...' – Additional Personnel to End of 1975

4   More of the Same, and the Competition for Points, 1976–77   18
The President's Cup, and How the Points Were Won – The Newcomer's Cup – 'Black Sunday' – A Stand-in for Brian – Summer Youth Hostel, 1976: Blackboys, Beachy Head and Guestling – New Rides for Old – Summary of 1976

5   Project 'QUINTA' and the Club's Changing Fortunes   26
Project 'QUINTA' – Why Did Project 'QUINTA' Fail?

6   A Time for Consolidation, 1977–79   29
After Project 'QUINTA' – East Anglia, 1977 – Sussex Coast Tour, 1977 – The Dungeness 'Flat Stone' Award, 1977 – Additional Personnel to End of 1977 – New

Rides for All, Greater Club Involvement, and the Search for a New Club Room – Summer YH Venture, 1978 – Haunted Borley – Autumn YH Break, 1978 – Additional Personnel to End of 1978 – 1979: Dwindling Attendance and Leaderless YH Touring – Seventh Petts Wood Company Girl Guides Cyclists' Badge-Testing – The BHF London-to-Brighton Charity Event – The Rabbits Farm Incident, June 1979 – The Curse of the Borley Brickwork? – YH Extravaganza, 1979 – Additional Personnel to End of 1979

7 The Pinnacle Year, 1980 49

Introduction to 1980 – The Club Trailer Sponsored Ride – Devon and Cornwall: The First Setback – The Second 'Event' – A Close Thing – Green Wheels The Unofficial Green Street Green Cycling Club Magazine – The Rest of the Year – Gatwick Airport – Two Mini-Tours for 1980 – Additional Personnel to End of 1980

8 1981 – The Club's Heyday 60

Building New Rides on Past Strengths – YH Tour, Easter 1981 – The London-to-Brighton – Summer YH Tour: Colchester, Nedging Tye, 1981 – A Continuing Success – The 'Nine Counties' YH Tour, October 1981 – Additional Personnel to End of 1981

9 Ten Years of The Green Street Green Cycling Club, 1982–83 66

A Slightly Downward Trend – A New Vigour for 1982 – Return of the Time-Trial – Marsh Green, Edenbridge – The Club's Tenth Anniversary Reunion – The Ten Per Cent Club – Guest of Honour – The 'Ten Counties' YH Tour, October 1982 – Introduction to 1983 – Kent–Surrey YH Tour, August 1983 – A Promising New Lease of Life: The Green Street Green Recruitment Drive, Summer 1983 – The Departure from Keston – The Club's New Venue: The Saxon Centre, Orpington – Additional Club Personnel to End of 1983

10 A New Era for the Club: 1984–87   90
*Introduction to 1984 – A Change of Direction –
Maintaining the Profile – Additional Personnel to End
of 1984 – The 'Calm Before the Storm', 1985 – YH
Drive, 1985 – And the Band Played Up ... – Additional
Personnel to End of 1985 – The Downturn, 1986–87 –
Leaner Times Ahead – Additional Personnel to End of
1987*

11 The Last Bastions: 1988   101
*The Will to Continue – The LFCDA Charity Fund-
raiser/Summer YH Tour, 1988 – Last Hope? –
Additional Personnel to End of 1988*

**12 The Demise of the Green Street Green Cycling
Club: 1989–92**   104
*Introduction, 1989 - 1990–92 – Additional Personnel to
End of 1992 – Why the Demise? A Potted History –
The External Factors – In Conclusion*

Epilogue   112
*A Green Street Green Cycling Club MK II? – Quotes
From Former Members*

**Appendix I: A Listing of Regular Club Outings
and YH Tours**   117
*Club Outings, 1972–91 – Club Youth Hostel Tours,
1974–88 – President's Cup Winners: Spring 1975 –
Summer 1988 – Newcomer's Cup Winners: 1977–83*

Appendix II: A Glossary of Popular Loakesisms   122
*Every Cyclist's Essential Roadside Guide to Club Ride
Survival*

Bibliography   125

LIST OF FIGURES

Figure 1	A certain Green Street Green Cycling club founder with his New Hudson at Albany Park, *c* 1945	2
Figure 2	Early club rides: Brian, Sheila – first club run, Dartford Heath, 1972	3
Figure 3	The club had barely begun but just look at that speed! David Wilkinson races his Dawes Red Feather over Dartford Heath 1972	3
Figure 4	Dartford Heath, 1972–73	4
Figure 5	GSGCC membership card	5
Figure 6	*Newsshopper* publicity piece, April 1973	6
Figure 7	GSGCC sew-on club badge	7
Figure 8	YH Colchester, February 1975	15
Figure 9	President's Club plinth detailing winners	19
Figure 10	'Black Sunday': site of accident	21
Figure 11	*Newsshopper* advert for stand-in leader, May 1976	22
Figure 12	Project 'QUINTA' paperwork	28
Figure 13	Six go to Dungeness Beach, YH tour, summer 1977	31
Figure 14	Keston Scout hut, the Club room site, 1978–84	34
Figure 15	Club fund-raising at Beech Road, 1978	36
Figure 16	Parents' excuse me/thank you notes, summer 1978	38

Figure 17	Greenstreet Green/Great Bricett misnomer	40
Figure 18	Girl Guides' Cyclist Badge paperwork	44
Figure 19	Robin Mazinke, 1979	47
Figure 20	Sponsored ride (for club trailer), 1980	50
Figure 21	Sharing a joke: Devon and Cornwall tour, Summer 1980	51
Figure 22	*Green Wheels* magazine, 1980	54
Figure 23	Some of the posters, ads and general publicity used by Green Street Green Cycling Club to attract new members	69
Figure 24	Ten-year anniversary 'natter and nosh' do, 1982 (tickets, replies, newspaper publicity/cuttings etc)	73
Figure 25	The author in pensive mood outside Tanners Hatch Youth Hostel, August 1983 tour	83
Figure 26	Brian's plea note to the club, 1983	86
Figure 27	The Saxon Centre, Orpington, the new Club room from 1984	88
Figure 28	Start of 'Ten Counties' tour, Autumn 1984	92
Figure 29	Toby Walter (with his Raleigh Record) watches as Mark Stowham has the locals eating out of his hand at Flatford Mill, August 1984	92
Figure 30	Smoky Loakes and crew, start of Arundel, 1985	95
Figure 31	Norman Park Carnival: roller demo, August 1986	97

Figure 32	The heavy snowfalls of 1986-87 had done much to quash hopes of winter cycling activity. Note the bus stop Brian had had erected in his front garden. The bus stop itself, formerly of West Kingsdown, had been uprooted during a Club ride and transplanted to Brian's driveway in May 1983	98
Figure 33	Barnstaple recruit: Abigail Treen *c* 1990	106
Figure 34	Worlds End Tour: founder, Brian Loakes, atop his 1990 Strada Carrera during 1993	111
Figure 35	Wedding photos of former club members Litton and MacInnis – now both Brown!	116

FOREWORD

Every now and again there comes a time in our lives when we are forced by some happening or occasion to take stock and look back at events that have had a direct bearing on our personal destiny. One such pleasant, thought-provoking moment descended upon me whilst reading this delightful cameo of the history of the Green Street Green Cycling Club.

The warmth of Philip Turner's graphic, tongue-in-cheek and easy-to-read style of writing paints pastel shades of many happy days awheel, evoking fond memories of my own cycling activities from everyday club life to the Tour de France...

Brian 'Smoky' Loakes shuffled into my life (he never walks!) more than 20 years ago, clutching a postcard that he wanted me to display in the window of my bike shop: an advertisement for a newly formed cycling club. I use pseudonyms for many of the characters that come into my establishment and Brian's appendage emanated from an obscure 1960s jazz tune entitled *Smoky Mokes*.

His other nickname of 'mean-Brian', mentioned in the text of this book, strikes me as somewhat harsh ... *careful* maybe, but certainly never mean.

His altruistic nature shines through the pages and over 500 people will owe him a lifelong debt for introducing them to the wonderful world of cycling – how can they ever repay him?

Ken Bird
June 1995

xiii

ACKNOWLEDGEMENTS

I would like to acknowledge the following for their assistance in the preparation of this work:

Ken Bird of Ken Bird Cycles, Green Street Green

St Mary's Church Centre for permitting me the unrequested, and invariably exclusive, use of their car park whilst going through the volumes of club records and memorabilia at Brian's house

Several former club members whose memories have helped lend the book some colour

To Brian, for reading the typescript through several times and often at short notice

To the late 'Mrs L.', Brian's wife, for her intuition in realising that helpings of tea and cakes would be very much the dietary requirement throughout the project

And to the following sponsors in particular: Youth Hostels Association (England & Wales), A.E. Smith (Joinery & DIY, High Street, Green Street Green), and Mrs R. Castle

The front cover photograph is reproduced courtesy of Renie Loakes; the back cover photograph is the author's own.

INTRODUCTION

Green Street Green Cycling Club was the creation of Brian Loakes. It was a club that had begun almost by accident; however, by the end of its 20-year run it had attracted some 530 members and had covered in excess of 207,000 collective miles during the course of its 100-plus popular cycle routes out of Green Street Green. It was a club that had enrolled a large section of the Green Street Green and wider community, introduced many to the enjoyable pastime of cycling, and afforded some couples the opportunity to meet and in a few cases actually to marry. Almost everybody in the Bromley Borough will have heard of the club, or at least known of someone who was a member at one time and, for sure, there were teenagers from as far afield as Penge, Sundridge and Shirley, and even one from Barnstaple in Devon, who knew its influence.

Many of us joined and remained active club members for about two or three years each, and during that time participated in many regular weekend cycle trips, as well as a few of the 30-odd week-long youth hostelling holidays that were organised.

So why a history of a club for which the last five or so years had seen something of a marked decline, a dwindling membership, and which had not in fact undertaken a single cycle trip in its last year? To answer that we need to go back to the beginning, to the club's genesis, and to chart its progress and development throughout the highs and lows of the 1970s and early 1980s, and to discover what the club had meant to the people who'd joined.

We believe that any and everybody who was a member of Green Street Green Cycling Club deserves a mention within the following pages, if only in passing, and for this we make little apology. It was the personalities of the members that contributed to making the club quite what it was – and, besides, how many other local cycle outfits could boast a roll-call of namesakes featuring among them a Mike Yarwood, an Oliver Reed, a Dean Martin, a Jerry Adams, a Frank Muir, a Paul Young or indeed a Terry Sullivan?

It is hoped that this brief history of the club will interest all past members – whether active or passive - as well as many of the parents and family and friends who watched from the sidelines, and indeed anybody else who knew of the club's existence and would wish to cherish its memory.

Philip Turner, 1995

1

The Club's Founder

The earliest memories would have to begin with Brian Loakes, who was born in Horton Kirby, near Dartford. By about 1944, at the age of eleven, he had begun to explore many local towns on his bike, a New Hudson (Figure 1), a single-speed roadster boasting rod brakes and 26 by 1⅜ inch wheels and which had cost him the princely sum of £8 19s 5d (a lot of money in those days and a far cry from the extravagance of his recent luxury ten-speed racer, a Dawes Five Star). The daily ride to school, near Crittalls Corner, only three miles away in Foots Cray, was one thing, yet he still recalls the severe 'choking off' he received from his mother upon telling her he'd cycled as far as Croydon and noting that he'd seen the trams. School holidays would see Brian making use of the Woolwich ferry to take in the East End areas of Silvertown and Poplar, and then also into Essex to explore Romford, Barking and Hornchurch. Riding south, he would extend his trips to the salubrious destinations of Sutton and Kingston as well as local Kentish areas as Dartford Heath in which in one incident in 1948 the treasured Hudson – his 'wings' – met with an unexpected ditch followed by sudden demise and an even longer walk home. Undeterred, Brian carried on with the business of cycling and would make use of many different models of bike up to and including well into his married life.

Figure 1 A certain Green Street Green Cycling club founder with his New Hudson at Albany Park, c 1945

The Early Rides, 1972–74

As has been mentioned in the Introduction, Green Street Green Cycling Club was never actually planned. However, it began in the late summer of 1972 when Sheila (Brian's eldest daughter) invited Brian along with her then boyfriend David Wilkinson to Dartford Heath (Figure 2, 3) and, following the success of the outing, decided next time they would ask along one or two others from their respective Charterhouse Road and Cray Valley schools. The first official 'club' ride, then, is recorded as taking place on Sunday, 17 September 1972 and comprised a total of seven members (Figure 4). Much of the credit for the club's early development must surely go to Sheila Loakes (now Sheila Bareham), who would be quick to pose the rhetorical question: 'Why don't we call ourselves the Green Street Green Cycling Club?'

The very next ride was advertised by word of mouth for

Figure 2 Early club rides: Brian, Sheila – first club run, Dartford Heath, 1972

Figure 3 The club had barely begun but just look at that speed! David Wilkinson races his Dawes Red Feather over Dartford Heath, September 1972

Figure 4 Dartford Heath, 1972–73

18 October and now included eight members: Sheila, David and Brian, along with five local newcomers, Bryan Wilkinson, Harvey Grainger, Colin Doolan, the late Danny Wilkinson and Mitchell Layng, and took them to Sevenoaks' Knole Park. Then 31 October saw a ride to Crystal Palace and a drop in membership to seven, following the departure of Mitchell (one wonders if he is still at Knole Park?).

However, the first indications that a club of some permanence was forming would occur during the fourth ride, in which one John Wright, a bus-driver colleague of Brian's who'd been busy organising his own local section of the CTC, persuaded him to join them on one of their trips to Wrotham. The 'planned merger', however, was never really to be, there being a clash of personality between Green Street Green and the CTC. Brian recalls a marked seriousness about the way he observed the CTC being run, which must have shaped his early visions of the new club's development: '*They [the CTC] appeared particularly regimental in their execution of stopping points and rest periods, and I recall there was to be strictly no overtaking the leader at any time – something I felt would have proved unpopular with some of our members who frequently enjoyed the almost continual "jockeying for position".'*

There can be little doubt that that meeting and the subsequent pressure to affiliate with – and inevitably to become swallowed by – the CTC had brought to the surface Brian's protective feelings towards the embryonic Green Street Green Cycling Club by urging him to produce the first official club membership cards for the rapidly sprawling membership (Figure 5). Ironically, and despite the initial lack of integration felt in riding with John Wright's CTC, a few further joint outings did take place in the summer of 1973.

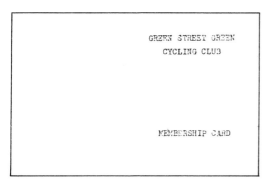

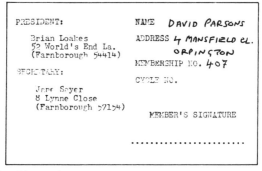

Figure 5   GSGCC membership card

By this time, too, the club had established itself through regular weekend rides to places such as Chipstead Lakes, Dartford Heath, Tonbridge and Long Reach – a further milestone being realised when, on a ride to Horton Kirby, club membership had seen a 50 per cent rise from 12 to 18, and due in no small part perhaps to the publicity given the club by the *Newsshopper* in April 1973 (Figure 6). Membership was now up to 23, with newcomers joining from as far afield as the Orpington districts of St Paul's and St Mary Cray.

Figure 6 *Newsshopper* publicity piece, April 1973

Perhaps one of the biggest influences at that time came by way of member number 30, Susie Litton (now Susie Brown), who, in Brian's words: '*added new vigour to the club by way of her enthusiasm and personality. She was in regular attendance, a keen cyclist and went on to become an early Green Street*

Green Cycling Club secretary'. That she was also just one of only two girls in a predominantly male-oriented cycling club was something of a novelty, and yet there was always the possibility that she would be able to attract and increase the female contingent. She did, by one, with a girl called Jenny Armour, who designed the club motif employed for its badges and T-shirts during its rapid expansion in 1975 (Figure 7).

Figure 7 GSGCC sew-on club badge

Interestingly, Jenny had joined Green Street Green Cycling Club in 1974 yet had only undertaken her first – and very nearly last – ride almost a year later in February 1975 when

Brian eventually procured her first bike for her – the practicalities of whether or not one needed a bike as a prerequisite for joining Green Street Green Cycling Club could be a mere detail in Brian's book!

However, it should be quite apparent by this time that it was indeed the women who were shaping the club – and had been from the very beginning: Sheila in suggesting the very idea and then name; Susie for injecting into the club drive, vigour and organisation; and then Jenny in providing the club its emblem, a one-dimensional bicycle wheel fimbriated in gold on a green background. It seems it was merely for the lads to turn up and get the pedals turning, end of story.

Key Personnel, 1972–74

Anthony Boughton, John Goslitski, Graham Garnett, Alison Loakes, Keith Wern, Chris Povall, Mark Beard, Debbie 'Cuddles' Smith, Martin Rourke, Chris Thompson, Garry Symmons, Paul and David Barsby, Gillian Lock and Dawn Phillips, Mick Baxter, Philip Norman, Andy Jordan, Tim Palmer, Philip Harvey, Keith Anderson, Geoff Cooper, Terry Crawley, Kevin Brown, Barry Sargeant, Barry and Eddie Sinfield, Paul Mortimer, Andy McClelland, Mark Mumbray, Michael Donovan, Peter Lorman, Colin Boucher, Derek and Neil Haggertay, Rory Cosgrove, Ricky Lacaille, Neville Roberts, Trevor Roseman, John Thorn, Philip Browne, Paul Rose and David Style.

2

Up and Running and Gathering Speed

Longer Trips, Farther Afield, 1974–75

The year 1974 saw further advances in club activity with the undertaking of longer rides and a party of six completing the 85-mile round trip to Southend that same July. New members for 1974 included Keith Anderson and Kevin Brown, Stephen Fosker, Mike Thorogood and Ian Humphrey.

By November, the club had staged its first ever youth hostel trip, to Badby YH in Northampton. Again, this was not something Brian had consciously planned; in fact the trip had been suggested by local youth club worker Paul Riches, who drove them there in his own minibus. Ten of a group of eleven had spent two days cycling around Stratford-upon-Avon and Nether Heyford and comprised Colin Bush, Tim Turner, Mike Cocker, Keith Howkins, Kevin Walford, Gary Westcar, Andy Marchant, Steve Vernon, Bartley Iagoe and, of course, Brian. Only John Wilkinson remained in the minibus throughout, tempted, perhaps, by the free cigarettes and the relative warmth of the bus. However, far from the venture being unsuccessful, it is a pity that all Brian is able to recall is that it was cold and drizzling with the group ending up thoroughly soaked – but then, who else would be sufficiently deranged to lead a cycle party at such short notice to a previously unexplored county and in the middle of winter? What was significant was that the club had become established with a willing membership and yet without actually trying.

The Green Street Green Cycling Club 'Official' Club Room

Up until now, cycle rides had been arranged for 9.30 a.m., from either outside Brian's house in World's End Lane or from the grounds of the church hall directly opposite. However, the burgeoning membership – now more than 30 – had made it necessary for there to be a separate place to meet which would provide also some much needed time to talk about new rides, competitions and forthcoming youth hostel trips. Most pressing of all, though, a club room would provide a chance for the group to get to know each other better, away from the confines of the Loakes' front room, which, like a majority of semi-detached houses, was never designed to hold more than about a half-dozen in comfort. A solution was found in an offer from Paul Riches, again (via club member 40 Kevin Ely), to make use of the annexe to St Giles' Church Hall in Church Road at Farnborough, about two miles from World's End Lane. Meetings would be arranged and held there free of charge beginning on Wednesday nights, the first on 18 September 1974 – exactly two years since the club's inception. This situation was maintained satisfactorily until the club's relocation to Keston in 1978, in spite of the rector, John Druce, upsetting the smooth running by suggesting that a pound-a-week payment for the hall's use would be in order! The problem now seemed to be that whilst club attendance had been improving (to 30 or so a week), there were in fact more members turning up here than for the actual club rides.

'I remember [thinking at that time] that I was never entirely happy with the situation, because I'd not set out in the business of running a youth club.' Brian adds, *'The Club, after all, was about cycling, but I figured I would just have to get on and make the most of it. In retrospect, I think it would've been quite a job coping with a party of more than 30 cyclists on the road.'*

3

A Cycling Club Proper, 1975–76

Introduction to Time-Trialling and Cyclo-Cross

In the tradition of any expanding club, new adventures were sought and planned, and the first of these, cyclo-cross, was arranged in January 1975 by Kevin Ely, Ian and Andy Humphrey, Mike Thorogood and Tim Turner, using the neighbouring fields off the old church hall site at Farnborough. It seemed that no one venue was used twice, which was at least in keeping with the club's seeming incapacity to plan ahead. Later venues included the official part-field/part-track site at Rectory Lane in Foots Cray Meadows in which club member number 80, Warren Marks, had been declared the outright winner among the 11 participants. A general lack of volunteers along with the progressively warming weather dictated that cyclo-cross, as a club event, would be shelved indefinitely.

Taking its place was the measurably more popular time-trial, the first being staged on 17 February 1975, a five-mile route commencing halfway down River Hill, south of Knole, then on through Seal and Sevenoaks and finishing back at the River Hill starting-point. Club records show 15 to have started out on what had begun as a planned ride to Knole Park, although only 12 finished. They were: Kevin Ely and Ian and Andy Humphrey, Keith Howkins, Steve Grant and Martin Rand, Jeremy Devese, Andy Marchant, Simon Wilkinson, Nick Wise and Paul Baker. What was odd about the time-trial was that not even approximate times were recorded,

11

but instead the (equally obscure) winner would be announced as he who had completed the most circuits!

The next time-trial was planned for the school Easter holiday on 27 March but was cancelled due to snow (did we only just say the weather was improving?). The next one, held in June, was staged at the A21 ten-mile route used regularly by such clubs as the Sydenham Wheelers and 34th Nomads, and started at Wellbrook Road in Farnborough. The route ran down the A21 to the roundabout at Green Street Green, through Pratts Bottom and up to the Black Eagle public house at Badgers Mount roundabout, then back along the A21 to Farnborough Hill, bearing left along Shire Lane and coming to a halt at the junctions of Shire Lane and North End Lane opposite High Elms Golf-course.

Time-trials continued successfully and with a kind of ad hoc regularity throughout the year and up until 1979, with the fastest ever club time notched up by Derek Taylor (335) at 25 minutes and 29 seconds – not bad for a touring club. As proof that some of the trials had been keenly contested, witness that David Rumm had very nearly equalled this time (note *nearly equalled*: nobody actually *loses* at Green Street Green Cycling Club), recording 25 minutes 31 seconds and 25 minutes 32 seconds in July and August respectively. And during an entirely different event, on 17 April 1976, there were *two* joint winners and also a pair coming in at joint second! Best times here were recorded as:

Martin Rand and Steve Hedges at 25 minutes 32 seconds and
Mike Thorogood and Steve Grant at 26 minutes 39 seconds

At the other end of the scale, we have to note a particularly slow time of 50 minutes 34 seconds going to club member number 141 Michael Curd, although he may wish to take solace from the fact that several entrants didn't even finish, claiming to have lost their way *en route* – the emerging pattern should be quite clear by now; indeed, this could only happen at the Green Street Green Cycling Club!

Sponsored Rides, Club Badges and T-Shirts and the Forming of the Committee

Another indicator of the club's progress became apparent when Brian saw the need to delegate responsibility. After all, by now the club had attracted some 112 members. It had begun to accumulate funds, albeit modest amounts obtained from the collection of weekly subs and from the sale of sweets and other canteen provisions, and in any case it was felt it would increase member participation and be one less thing to worry about if a treasurer were appointed. The first Green Street Green Cycling Club Committee, then, looked as follows:

President:	Brian Loakes
Secretary:	Susie Litton
Treasurer:	Kevin Ely
along with a serving committee of six	

Under discussion during this and subsequent meetings were the perennial topics of new routes for the regular club rides and forthcoming YH tour plans; and also how to cope with the increasingly pressing problem of storage at the Farnborough club room (all items for club nights were having to be transported to the club room, unpacked from and subsequently repacked into cycle panniers, and then taken home again to be stored in Brian's garden shed); these committee meetings also served as a 'think tank' for any ideas for activities that would help boost club funds.

A Sponsored Ride for Club Badges

One of the first fund-raising activities held was a sponsored cycle ride from the George & Dragon public house at Farnborough, the committee having first devised a circuit measuring laps of 1.8 miles. The event took place on the evening of 23 April 1975, and then again on the following Monday for those who had been unable to make this. In total, £20 was raised, which was put toward the cost of the Green Street

Green Cycling Club badges that the committee had agreed would help raise the profile of the club and, besides, Brian figured that the money could be recovered by selling to members at little over cost (approximately 30p each). Reminiscent of a Byzantine tax fiddle, Brian had gone to considerable lengths to have the badges made by Cory's in the Republic of Ireland, where no VAT would be payable. All the more disappointing, then, that their cost would come to £21 – one pound more than the ride had been able to raise!

Capitalising on the success of the badges – the first batch had sold out prior to their arrival – plans were already afoot for a club T-shirt, a striking green-on-yellow design, the reverse of the badge, in fact, and one, it is believed, that can still be seen worn in local parts.

A review of some of the more recent ride destinations for the first half of 1975 included: Hampton Court (50 miles); Aylesford, near Maidstone (50); and Upnor Castle at Chatham (55); while regular, well-established outings now comprised a core of the following: Whipps Cross (40) and Yalding (50) – the former hosting the occasional rowing-boat excursion, while the latter sometimes a trip by motor boat– Tonbridge (35), Sevenoaks' Knole Park (20), Eynsford (15), Edenbridge (35) and Southend, which had boasted, at that time, a maximum attendance for any club ride: a party of 19.

Another point of note was that committee membership had expanded to ten, new members featuring: Tim Turner, Jenny Armour, Robert O'Dwyer and Charlie Crayford. It was during one of the new committee's by now frequent meetings that the 'four-week rule' for new members was proposed. Brian's memory appears somewhat hazy on this point, although it is considered to have been a requirement that any new recruit undergo a limited probationary period and participate in a minimum number of rides before he or she could be considered to have officially joined. Again, this could well have been linked to the trend that while membership was still spiralling, the same was not being reflected in the numbers active in taking up weekend rides. How far the new rule was enforced, or indeed could be enforced, is not entirely clear.

'Time, Gentlemen, Please...'

The latter part of 1975 did not see quite the kind of activity witnessed during the first half of the year. The highlight, however, was the second YH trip. (The first of the year took place in Colchester in February, Figure 8.) This led the club

Figure 8 YH Colchester, February 1975

to the south coast, staying one night at Guestling and two at Beachy Head on the weekend of 29–31 August and also took in a ride to Brighton, the later preferred destination for club outings to coincide with the annual London-to-Brighton British Heart Foundation charity fund-raising event, beginning in 1976. It would probably be fair to say that no Green Street Green Cycling Club outing was complete without a calamity of some sort, and this time it was the turn of Andrew Grier, who, having every intention of completing his first youth hostel run with the club, regrettably had to return after the five or so miles that took the party of eight to Polhill, where he emptied his entire stomach contents at the roadside. (Was the prospect of three whole nights away with the club really so bad?) In the true spirit of generosity, however – indeed by now the club's very stock-in-trade – Andrew *was* awarded the half-mileage point he'd earned in coming this far and had no points deducted for holding the party up while all waited for a car to take both him and his bike home.

That Brian might have found this more amusing than most, and also that he had been instrumental in fabricating the night-time 'ghost stories' during the recent hostel trip, required that he undergo a bringing-down-to-earth experience. And one happened to him somewhat sooner than expected. It was during another of the CTC tie-ins along with junior section leader John Wright, in which an 'up-market' picnic to the Ashdown Forest had been planned. Brian, ever keen to impress over the club's rapid expansion and, with it, acceptance wherever they went, surely had to conceded a club point or two when he was refused entry to the pub to celebrate with a round of drinks. This, Brian was told, and in full view of John Wright, had to do with his appearance (cycle attire, he insists) and that the pub did not want to attract 'that sort of clientele'. Possibly this had been the club's first major set-back!

The remaining quarter of the year saw many rides cancelled due to poor weather, and indeed there was little club activity in general. However, as a result of increasing funds, the club was able to make a small contribution toward the reconstruction of the recently burned-down local Scout hut, which was to be relocated in Highfield Avenue. On an equally low-key note, the year concluded with Robert O'Dwyer replacing Susie Litton as Club Secretary, a post he maintained until January 1977.

Additional Personnel to End of 1975

Stephen Sinfield, Billy Manser, Mike Austin, Paul Britten, Christopher Pitt, Mark, Paula and Claire Bushnell, Tim Austin, Anthony Ferrier, Paul Fallick, Chris Parkin, Paul Hailes, Bryan Massey, George and Jim Bryant and Stephen and Anthony Burt, Peter Aley, Alan Ryder, Martin Rayner, Simon Ellis, Neil McGrath, Shaun Burbeck, Marcus Meadows-Smith, Steve Hedges, Paul Williams, Mark Lavelle, Gregory Bennett, John Corteen, Chris Branch, Mick Beale, Mark Kingswood, Mark Sommer, Dean Martin, Glenn Harrold and Glenn (Guy) Salmon, Les Williams, David Noble, David Rydell and Denise O'Dwyer.

4

More Of The Same, and the Competition for Points, 1976–77

The President's Cup, and How the Points Were Won

January 1976 saw something of a slight decline in club night attendance, from around 30 members the year before to approximately 20, a trend that persisted for about six months. In a bid to win back the falling club attendance (which, if left to subside in this way, would no doubt have had an important bearing on the weekend ride attendance figures), the President's Cup was introduced. This was a trophy that would be presented biannually by Brian to the member contributing most to the club during that period, be it in the form of regular weekend outings and youth hostel tours, for which a mileage point would accrue for every ten miles a member cycled, or club attendance on Wednesday nights (a point was even awarded for turning up now); and at other functions, such as the Green Street Green Summer fête and Norman Park's annual Bromley Carnival at which Green Street Green Cycling Club would show a regular presence, points would be awarded according to hourly attendance. Now if all this sounds a little manipulative in maintaining members' interest and participation in the club, then it was a gamble that paid off. Indeed, the cup played an integral part in encouraging club activity right up until its (the cup's) discontinuation in 1988.

Figure 9 portrays the President's Cup and lineage of winners from 1975 to 1988.

Figure 9 President's Club plinth detailing winners

The Newcomer's Cup

If the President's Cup was introduced in order to help sustain the interest and activities of established club members then another, token, cup was also considered a necessary incentive for similar interest and competition amongst new members. Consequently, the Newcomer's Cup was introduced in 1977, with points being earned in precisely the same manner as for the President's Cup. There is little doubt that this cup, too, was instrumental in maintaining the interest of new members in Green Street Green Cycling Club as well as fostering the competitive spirit. In the words of one former club member: *'With already many known previous cup winners, along with the fulfilment rides would bring, incentive to try and compete for either cup would have been great.'*

A full listing of President's and Newcomer's Cup winners can be found in Appendix I.

'Black Sunday'

On Sunday 9 May – or 'Black Sunday' as many early club members will recall – an incident occurred on what was an otherwise routine outing to Long Reach, Dartford Marshes. It resulted in leader Brian Loakes being knocked from his bike, a much valued Alan Shorter, and being taken to Dartford's West Hill Hospital with a broken collar-bone, bruises and mild grazing, plus approximately £130 worth of rebuilding needed to repair the damage the bike had suffered. It needed a further six weeks of convalescence to restore Brian, during which a new, temporary, leader had to be found to stand in.

The incident itself began on the return journey from Long Reach as the club descended Temple Hill, near Dartford Station, and approached Overy Street, an adjoining side-road. At the very junction, Brian was struck side-on by the driver of a rusty light metallic green saloon (and what else if not matching the description of an everyday early 1970s BL/ Austin?), who had failed to stop at the dotted white lines.

CYCLIST HURT.—Mr Brian Victor Loakes (43), of Worlds End Lane, Green Street Green, was treated at West Hill Hospital, Dartford, for a broken collar-bone after his cycle had been involved in a collision with a car at the junction of Mill Pond Road and Overy Street, Dartford, on Sunday. The car driver, Mr Pargat Singh Bhogal, of Dartford, was unhurt.

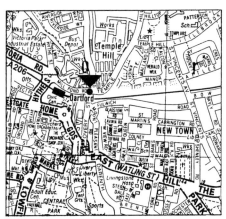

Figure 10 'Black Sunday': site of accident

Figure 10 depicts the 'Black Sunday' black spot which for some time afterwards must have sent a shiver down the collective club spine when it was remembered that the loss of its founding leader could have brought about the club's early demise. In passing, it is perhaps worth noting that around £30 worth of damage had also been done to Club Secretary Rob O'Dwyer's treasured five-speed Raleigh Olympus, bringing the total damage to around £160 – a lot of money in 1976!

A Stand-in for Brian

Undaunted, and ever keen to have the club back on the road, Brian arranged that same week for an ad (Figure 11) to be placed in the local *Newsshopper* for a temporary cycle club leader, the requirement being for somebody of sufficient maturity to lead the cycle party on successive weekend rides, and also to stand in at the regular Wednesday night club get-togethers.

NEWS SHOPPER

ORPINGTON & CHISLEHURST   16 Editions Delivered Weekly to 520,000 Greater London H

Cyclist Wanted

THE Green Street Cycling Club, which has been in operation for three years, caters for youngsters between the ages of 11 and 16. Unfortunately, the organiser, Mr. Loakes, has had an accident and is unable to lead the youngsters for about six weeks. He would like to hear from anyone who would be willing to lead the youngsters for this period. Please Ring Farnborough 54414. U96

Figure 11   *Newsshopper* advert for stand-in leader, May 1976

In the three or so weeks that this took to arrange, a local applicant by the name of Steve Mott, a regular racing merchant (and not a tourer), led a somewhat diminutive party of two to a destination the club records show as Eastway Racing Track at Leytonstone on 30 May. The very small turn-out, coupled with the fact that Mr Mott would prefer a racing to touring mode, meant that this was his first and only association with Green Street Green Cycling Club. The club was still saddled (pun contrived) with the problem of finding a replacement for the very temporary leader who had only just joined.

Sometimes the most obvious solutions are the last to be realised, because the gap was eventually filled by old party hand Susie Litton, who had in fact resigned over a year before in 1975. Mercifully she stepped back into the fold, fulfilling the role of acting president from 6 June to 8 July, sufficient to assure the continuation of club rides and flagging morale until Brian could resume his presidency. Rides during this interim period broke no really new ground, but instead stayed close to the tried-and-tested favourites of Tonbridge (twice), Wateringbury, Tunbridge Wells, Yalding, Shoreham and Hampton Court. Well done, Susie!

Summer Youth Hostel, 1976: Blackboys, Beachy Head and Guestling

The summer holidays saw the club on a return visit to the south coast hostels over the period 29 July to 3 August. Club personnel were drawn up from a contingent of five: Brian and Rob O'Dwyer, Mick Beale and Ben Myram, with Stewart Pettet making his own way down for the first night's stopover at Guestling. It was now becoming a commonplace on club YH tour departure day, for a brace of non-hostel-bound riders to come with the club to a pre-arranged point on the ride, thereby making for a halfday's outing and the opportunity to earn those valuable President's Cup-winning points. That day's complement was club member number 43, Mike Thorogood, and 74, Brian Altimas, who'd ridden with the party to as far as Tonbridge.

New Rides for Old

August 1976 saw a new ride – albeit to a destination that would have been more appropriate for October – to All Hallows, on the south side of the Thames Estuary. When asked whether, at that time, there had ever been pressure to invent a greater variety of club rides, Brian argued that actual destination had never been, and *should* never be, a major issue in determining attendance numbers, and that most members were merely riding for the sheer pleasure and benefits that club cycling could offer. Furthermore, Brian pointed out, even if they had cycled to a restricted number of destinations in fairly rigid rotation, there would always be somebody new to the club who'd not previously been with them and, on that basis, no two rides could ever really be compared. To that end, the actual ride destination point could be consideredly largely irrelevant. Additionally, the club had gone on to enjoy a good 20-year run of cycling highs and lows, and in that time only 108 different ride routes (though not including regular YH touring schedules) had been officially recorded, which was telling of the club's attitude towards the business of cycling. The determination to use every available weekend, half-day or evening to maximum effect was exemplified by the frequent, and often short-notice, arrangements for brief youth hostel runs such as the one that took them to Guestling during the half-term of October 1976.

Another new ride (later referred to as 'the bonfire ride', taking the club around the Biggin Hill/Downe and High Elms areas) was initiated on 5 November, after which the group recall returning to Brian's house in World's End Lane for a treat of 'bomb tatties' – Loakesspeak for jacket potatoes. To know what to expect on a Green Street Green outing would have been something!

A recurring source of mystery for the club, however, was that whilst Brian would always ensure a club presence at community events such as summer fêtes and church hall Christmas bazaars, the club would rarely, if ever, manage to attract new membership there. This was all the more surprising, considering the scores of local people that these happenings would inevitably bring together. It was a similar story in later years whenever the club advertised for members in newspapers and free sheets or via posters displayed on the walls of library, community college, school and sports club halls; indeed, it did seem a particularly regular pattern for recruits to have been drawn, almost to a member, exclusively from the schools and by the word-of-mouth referral of school friends and acquaintances.

Summary of 1976

In summarising 1976, [the club diary records] that membership had topped 180 by the year's end, up 55 on the previous year (with club attendance in June fixing a record high of 33), and with a fairly consistent 'active' body of about 45. This membership would remain loyal for several years until about the time of the club's tenth anniversary celebrations in 1982. When asked about the year's progress, Brian remarked that 'Black Sunday' apart, he would be happy to carry on the next year as before, now that the club was achieving manageable numbers and what was, after all, a fairly strong following. Repeated reference was made to the problems likely to arise from any plan to expand the club in that, as before, any extra responsibility would simply fall to Brian.

In the meantime, however, there were plans afoot to turn the village of Green Street Green into a very magnet for cycle activity. Local cycle shop entrepreneur Ken Bird had put together an ambitious proposal to build a common club site for five separate cycling outfits of which Green Street Green Cycling Club would be one. This was known as Project 'QUINTA' and, had it been successful, would probably have changed the face and indeed, the very nature of the club forever.

5

Project 'QUINTA' and the Club's Changing Fortunes

.

Project 'QUINTA;

Project 'QUINTA', the brainchild of Green Street Green bike shop owner Ken Bird, involved the idea of bringing together five quite disparate local cycling clubs, namely Ken's own racing club, CC Orpington, Catford Cycling Club, the Sydenham Wheelers, the West Kent District Association of the CTC and Green Street Green Cycling Club, in order to build common premises, each occupying the club room for its own specific club meet nights (each assigned a different weekday evening), which would benefit all in terms of shared overheads; improved storage facilities for members' bikes and club possessions; and communal changing-room/shower facilities; cycle rollers and training machines; cycling videos and, later, satellite TV facilities, and even as a regular promotion point for any forthcoming local attraction. A further benefit would have come from the reservoir of potential newcomers who might avail themselves of any one or more of the 'new' clubs now at their disposal. Furthermore, each club would remain mutually independent of the others, there being little pressure to participate in any joint event other than the initial publicity for the venture; and so it was clear that all would benefit from a collective involvement. That the village of Green Street Green would have been transformed into a very byword for cycling would have had tremendous impact on Green Street Green Cycling Club, which, being the junior club in almost all respects, would have had most to gain. It is highly likely that the club would have gone from strength to strength and need never again have sought active recruitment for new members.

Why Did Project 'QUINTA' Fail?

On the fact of it, Project 'QUINTA' had much going for it: all the advantages listed above, plus a wealth of cheap, ready labour, a choice of (free) sites and the pledge that the London Borough of Bromley would match, pound for pound, the input of the newly formed consortium. It was Ken Bird's estimate that, even without council backing, it would still be possible for the project to raise in the order of £50,000. Furthermore, the site could be up and running inside five years, that is, by about 1982.

There was the fear – real or imagined – that by forming a union with like clubs, some of them might lose their identities. Others, it was argued, felt their members already had to travel far enough on club nights and that the extra mileage (particularly during winter) would be sufficient to render their participation impracticable.

Others still felt the co-existence of so many clubs would mean running the risk of having their members poached by another, but it could be counter-argued that there would be a greater pool of newly attracted members from which to enrol, in addition to the fact that, in time, each club would develop its own membership potential.

By far the greatest problem that beset the launch of 'QUINTA' seemed, sadly, to be that of apathy, particularly on the part of the Catford and Sydenham Wheelers clubs, the latter defeating the proposal by a margin of a single vote.

Ken Bird: '*[Project] "QUINTA" could have provided the means to focus a tight cohesive cycle organisation had the clubs with the largest clout been able to think sufficiently big'*.

Inter-club debate over Project 'QUINTA' occupied some ten months until its collapse in October 1977. Some of the paperwork can be seen in Figure 12.

Our Ref./INVOICE No. ....

Your Ref./INVOICE No. ....

TO WHOM IT MAY CONCERN.

Are you happy with your present Clubroom? ''Is it dank and lifeless? Do you play 'second fiddle' to the Girl Guides or Boy Scouts?

LET'S GET TOGETHER!!

For far too long many Clubs in this area have had to 'make do' with less than ideal facilities for their members. As a group we cyclists do not ask much of our community but we do sell ourselves short and end up paying for other people's pleasures such as the 'Churchill Theatre' or the 'Walnuts Sports Centre. Why should we have to accept third rate when other more vociferous or powerful groups of people demand (and get) first-class everything ......

LET'S HELP OURSELVES!!

We would like to put forward an idea that could place five Clubs on the map in the Orpington area and set cycling on a footing that would no longer be something of a music hall joke.

"PROJECT QUINTA"

The basic idea is that a group of five go-ahead Clubs link up to sponsor and build its own clubhouse (each Club would retain its own individual identity). This would be a purpose built cycling clubhouse with all the various facilities that cyclists and only cyclists need. Just think of some of the advantages! A bike annexe to keep your machine safe and out of the rain; billiards and table tennis; a library of maps, books and touring aids; rollers and weight-training 'gear'; a stage from which to run dances and discos; central heating; lower Club subs; communal printing facilities; a good kitchen; inside toilets and showers, etc. etc. You could even use the place to run your own Club dinners (think how much that alone would save!)

Registered Office : 35 HIGH STREET, GREEN STREET GREEN, ORPINGTON, KENT.   V.A.T. Reg. No. 206 6087 74

Figure 12 Project 'QUINTA' paperwork

6

A Time for Consolidation, 1977–79

After Project 'QUINTA'

If 1976 had seen opportunity for great change within Green Street Green Cycling Club, then 1977 saw a return to the form of old with the continuation of regular club rides and youth hostel trips, and a steadily growing membership.

The club began 1977 with a keen interest in Project 'QUINTA', with Brian, Martin 'Evil Mac' McAuley and Jeremy Gurton acting as club ambassadors and periodically visiting the other clubs' venues for special site meetings. There is little doubt that whilst the breadth of the club's influence might have been relatively insignificant (compared with, say, Bird's own CC Orpington, who were small in numbers but renowned internationally for their racing prowess), by generating high membership numbers and enthusiasm they would have more than compensated.

East Anglia, 1977

The school Easter holiday period saw the first youth hostel break of 1977, taking a group of seven (Brian, Adrian Self, Stewart Pettet, 'Evil Mac', Phil Turner, Adam 'Tiny Tim' Winter and Keith Howkins) on a tour of East Anglia with stopovers at Colchester, Nedging Tye and Castle Hedingham. Between the two nights at Colchester, seaside jaunts were arranged to Clacton and Felixstowe and also to Constable's Flatford Mill, taking in the picturesque Willy Lott's cottage and the fishing of eels from the Mill river. Many scenic and interesting sites were shown to the parties that toured regularly with the club and, asked to reflect on this particular period, Brian was quick to appreciate the direction the club had been taking. In fact, his statement might have summarised the club at almost any point during its 20-year history: *'There is something very pleasant, a certain unity, in leading a party of cyclists around different parts of England ... the motivation for me, while wanting to explore places that I'd [read] about, was to have had a membership with which to be able to share it all.'*

May 1977 saw Green Street Green's participation at the local fête – by now a regular means of raising club funds – with repeated use of the infamous home-made 'spinning-wheel' attraction (a bicycle wheel, with an arrow marked on a particular spoke and affixed to a backing board divided into 12 segments). When the wheel stopped spinning, the arrow would come to rest in one of the 12 sectors and the lucky winner make off with a bottle of Pomagne! The wheel became a regular attraction, earning a modest profit for club coffers time and again.

Sussex Coast Tour, 1977

From 29 August to 3 September there was a return to the club's 'residency' on the Sussex coast, taking in three nights at Guestling YH and two at Beachy Head. Keen to give value for money (and providing for those who so wished a chance to earn extra President's Cup points), Brian continued the evening cycle runs, the first of which was to Fairlight. On 30 August the group of seven – Brian, Rob O'Dwyer, Martin and Mark McAuley, Phil Turner, Adrian Self and Jeremy Gurton – went to Dungeness via Romney Marsh and Lydd. Figure 13 shows a restless group playing with whole sections of derelict railway line and track and the remnants of an old truck – the kind of activity that would need early curtailment before somebody got hurt! Boredom was averted via an ascent up the nearby lighthouse.

Figure 13 Six go to Dungeness Beach, YH tour, summer 1977

The next day took the group on a trip inland to Bodiam Castle (as a welcome change to the daily coastal runs that inevitably took place during these hostel visits) but *was* it mere coincidence that daytime routes would invariably pass the site of a derelict building or disused length of railway line? Certainly, as far as Brian's personal interests were concerned, a pattern was beginning to emerge for anybody able to read between the lines! Daytime rides for the remainder of the tour took in the nearby Hastings seafront, followed by the A259 coastline route to Beachy Head and Eastbourne, after that Brighton, and then home again via Southwater BR station – site of another disused railway line.

The club sponsored ride this year took place in November and saw 12 take part, along with a non-cycling contingent of one – Brian. £58 was raised, which would go toward purchase of further stocks of club T-shirts and also the necessary materials to build a much wanted full-sized table-tennis table.

The year also saw growing confidence within the club members themselves. Mark 'Plastic Mac' McAuley and Phil Turner arranged the first solo YH outing, including a stopover in the sub-zero chill of Kemsing's hostel annexe one Friday night and then Doddington on the Saturday – a choice of hostel that would prove a particular favourite for the club in future tours. Club spirit was fortified by a pre-arranged meeting of the duo by members Loakes, Jem Gurton, Tim Cross and Peter Sears at the familiar Tunbridge Wells Toad Rock at midday on Sunday. This first solo tour did not in any way threaten a breakaway, as might have been anticipated; in fact, if anything, it showed the way for future deputy leadership should Brian ever find himself indisposed at short notice. Phil, fairly active within the group until 1979, went on to lead further YH shorts during 1978 along with fellow club member Martin McAuley, to hostels Overton, Oxford and Ivinghoe in June, and then again in August and September with Kane 'Stick' Mayhook, taking in Goudhurst, Truleigh Hill and Holmbury St Mary.

The Dungeness 'Flat Stone' Award, 1977

As already noted, both 1976 and 1977 had sparked off an era which would see healthy competition to collect the mileage (and club night attendance) points necessary to stand a chance of winning the President's and Newcomer's cups. However, in 1977 a particular one-off award was made for an event that had occurred during the return journey from Beachy Head youth hostel when Rob O'Dwyer's back tyre burst. Rob, judging the tyre to be beyond immediate repair, continued to ride the remaining 17½ wheel-buckling miles with the tyre completely flat. The feat was commemorated by inscription on a large flat stone which Brian had picked up only days earlier on Dungeness Beach.

Several small, yet nonetheless significant, improvements were made to benefit the club night attendance, by way of a new dartboard and table tennis equipment and a better selection of confectionery offered in the canteen. On 28 December was the first of what was to become a regular year-end occurrence: the annual after-Christmas knees-up and left-overs bash at Brian's house in Worlds End Lane. It was attended at its launch by a particularly high turnout of 15 – cheaper than hiring a skip!

Additional Personnel to End of 1977

Russell Lea, Chris Jackson, Michael Pooley, Gary Thomas, Ashley Heming, Bradley Hill, Michael Davies, Simon Whitbread, Peter Stogdon, Kevin Cooper, Andrew Payne, Terry Popping, Bernard Cook, Colin Etheridge, John Davis, Dean and Wayne Nowers, Mark Fry, Anthony Lacroix, Ian Rowlan, Stephen Mack, Graham Young, Jeremy Lay, Michael Netherton, Garry Pulling, Terry Corcoran, John Hepburn, Gavin and Mark Rothwell, Stewart Dillaway, Robert Conroy-Finn, John Towers, John Easdown, David Thomas, Mark Smith, Tim Young, Peter Buxton, Mark Edwards, Stephen Hill, Paul Bennett, Jonathan and Brendan Roper, Paul Condon, Keith Brown, Gary Young, Chris Taylor, Paul Lyas, Michael Mee, Gerald Buckle, John Davies, Graham Silverton, Jim Sherwood, Morley Young, Alex Eade, Paul Young, Ian Harrison, Alastair Jamieson, Martin Gould, Michael Chandler, Bruce Cornford, Ian Furness, Paul Cohen, Barry Waller, Peter Sears, Paul Miller, Liz Sands, Marina Adinolfi, Paul Coulson, Gavin Emsden, Mark Bates, Rob Winter, Andy Coleman, Ian Heath, Terry and Tony Sullivan.

New Rides for All, Greater Club Involvement, and the Search for a New Club Room

The new year, 1978, kicked off with a local YH trip to Crockham Hill and Doddington for Mark McAuley, Tim

Cross, Adam Winter, Jem and Brian spanning 13–15 January. Winter touring for the club was something of a novelty, yet, considering its success, it went on to set a future trend. Doddington was a good winter choice for its open log fire and novel visitors' book, a kind of scrapbook, Brian recalls, comprising a collage of the hostel's own history.

Between February and March, Jem and Brian set about building the table tennis tabletop in two halves which, although constructed professionally, would eventually sit atop two old trestle-tables of non-regulation height. The construction of the table took only four weeks; however, in typical Green Street Green tradition, the table would really only see use upon the club's overnight departure from the St Giles's site to a new venue. This was the 17th Bromley Scout hut at Keston, situated on the Croydon Road and shared alongside the Sydenhams (Figure 14). Subs now rose by 50 per cent, although that was a small price to pay for improved storage facilities. The new table tennis feature was a welcome

Figure 14 Keston scout hut, the Club room site, 1978–84

addition, helping boost club attendance via the promotion of regular tournaments and competitions.

Wednesday, 31 May would be the last official club gathering to take place at the St Giles's annexe at Farnborough. Green Street Green had been well-established there, seeing the place as home for the last three seasons, and so it had come as something of a surprise for Brian to be suddenly given two weeks' notice to vacate the premises on the grounds of 'noise, rowdiness and general unruly behaviour' – although it was probably not too difficult to sympathise with this decision when one imagines the effect that two dozen or so boisterous teenagers might be having upon the place.

Holiday commitments meant the club would already be taking a few weeks off from meetings; however, this would still leave a lot of work to be done if new premises were to be acquired prior to June, when club nights would resume. All the more pressing, then, if the annual Southend ride (early June), the Green Street Green Summer Fête and yet another fund-raising event at Beech Road were to be included in the interim as well as a YH trip to Guestling/Beachy Head (comprising 'new' members Billy Cooper and Mark Bates along with regulars Tim Cross, Neil Emsden and Brian) at the end of May. In fact, several local sites had been considered – the majority being unsuitable for one reason or other, often boiling down to a usual lack of storage facilities, expensive rents or lack of available nights. Possible sites included: St Mary's Church Hall in Worlds End Lane and right opposite Brian's house (too expensive); the Greenwood Centre in Green Street Green High Street (no available nights); the Methodist Church Hall, Farnborough (limited storage space); St James's Hall at Crofton (lack of free nights, cost and storage!) and even the tin hut at the rear of The Plough public house on Bromley Common.

It did look as though time was running out for the club, until the Keston Scout hut opposite The Drift entrance to Ravenswood School was discovered, seeming to satisfy the club's requirements and at an affordable weekly rent. The only other change would be that club nights would switch to Thursdays.

It has to be said that opening night at the new venue brought with it poor attendance, a total of only nine bodies, and for this it was decided that *Top Of The Pops* would take much of the blame. However, a new era was dawning with the recruitment of Jo Gray (Matthew's sister) and her friend Samantha Thompson, who became member number 239.

This middle part of 1978 began what was, for Brian, the start of the 'Coopers' days', referring to the new members' school, where a following would be created. New Coopers' recruits went on to include: Fiona MacInnis, Sarah Stonham, Louise Wilson (who later married Jeremy 'Jem' Gurton the very same day, incidentally, that fellow recruit and friend Jo Gray married non-club member Rob Caiger), along with Beverley Smith, Angela Daws, Jane Sayer and Sarah John. This period showed a parallel with the 'Charterhouse days' of c. 1972–73 which had seen an equally similar intake of new members from Orpington's Charterhouse Road school.

Figure 15 Club fund-raising at Beech Road, 1978

The new club site brought a concomitant broadening of activity, particularly where fund-raising would be concerned. Green Street Green did not have to look too far for their next assignment, which found them shifting heaps of garden earth into a succession of skips (Figure 15) for local resident and club member Kane Mayhook's father, Len. The Green Street Green Summer Fête, held on 10 June, helped raise a further £20 and was attended by a 14-strong turnout, demonstrating the club members' recently renewed interest.

Within a matter of a few short weeks, club night attendance reverted to the levels previously enjoyed at St Giles's and, if further proof of the members' dedication to their club be needed, Figure 16 depicts a brace of 'excuse/thank you' notes written by some of the members' parents on their behalf during summer 1978.

Summer YH Venture, 1978

The summer YH tour of 1978 was booked for East Anglia again at the hostel favourites of Colchester, 28–30 July, and Nedging Tye, 31 July–2 August. The party of ten comprised the by now regular touring body of Brian, Jeremy Gurton, Tim Cross, Martin McAuley, Phil Turner and Neil Emsden, along with relative YH tour newcomers Matthew Gray, Jason Bonner, Kane Mayhook and Andy 'Bungle Bonce' Bunce. As was fast becoming the club custom, the party was again joined by latecomers. First, Jeremy, met at Marks Tey, ten miles south of Colchester, by Brian, Jason and Neil, who received a thorough drenching in the near day-long downpour (and thereby proving that not all had been lost); and also Martin McAuley, who had arranged to meet the group during the second leg of the tour at Nedging Tye. Club rides embraced a variety of destinations which, in addition to Clacton Pier, took in Ipswich and also a village named Great Bricett about a mile east of Nedging Tye. What was particularly noteworthy about the place was that on Brian's OS map of the Nedging Tye area (Figure 17), about a mile south of Bricett was printed the village of Greenstreet Green, and so it

01-462 ~~5886~~ 8786.

130 QUEENSWAY
WEST WICKHAM
KENT BR4 ODZ
May 13th 1948.

Dear Mr Noakes

Jason is very disappointed that he will not be able to go with you cycling tomorrow. (Sunday)

On Friday he had an accident on his cycle & I'm afraid his front wheel & fork were very badly buckled.

His Dad tried so hard to get the parts so he would be able to take part but had no luck getting the front fork. As soon as his bike is fixed he will be able to resume.

Yours Sincerely
J. Bonnel.

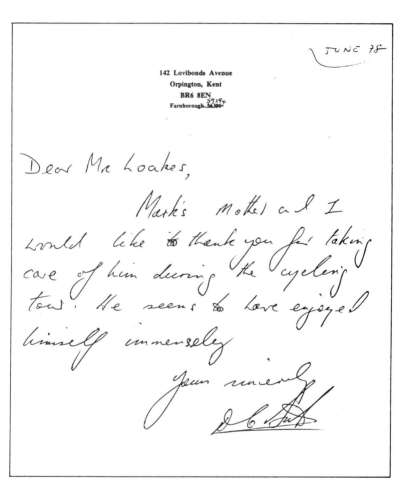

Figure 16 Parents' excuse me/thank you notes, summer 1978

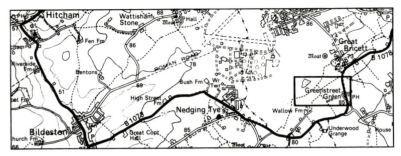

Figure 17 The Greenstreet Green/Great Bricett misnomer

was only natural that the namesake be sought out and photographed for posterity. What was surprising was the blanket denial by the half-dozen or so locals questioned that the village had ever existed, thereby quashing all hopes of a sister cycling club with which ours might have been able to identify.

Haunted Borley

Borley, another local Suffolk village, had acquired a reputation of having 'the most haunted house in England', according to a book written by Harry Price in 1940. The haunted house was in fact the nineteenth century-built rectory sited about a quarter of a mile from the church. There had been several reported instances of poltergeist activity, apports and sudden appearance of wall-writing, in addition to bells being caused to ring and the church organ playing of its own accord. By 1939 the rectory was destroyed by fire, an event itself foretold during a one-time ouija session and, despite the resultant rubble having been recycled for use in the construction of a new building, this one, too, had subsequently collapsed to the ground.

And so it was during the club visit to Borley in 1978 that Brian and Jason (Bonner) managed to retrieve a fragment of the brickwork. Shelving the artefact in his transport library cabinet at home, Brian flatly denied any connection with the demise of the Green Street Green Cycling Club some years later, although some might see it as more than just a little odd that the youth hostels of Tavistock and Hayle, Nedging Tye and Oddington, as well as Goudhurst, (let alone the Farnborough St Giles's annexe and, later, the Orpington Saxon Centre), should all have cause to be shut down or razed after even brief Green Street Green Cycling Club involvement ... very odd indeed.

The August Bank Holiday Carnival at Bromley's Norman Park found strong team support, as well as an increase in raffle sales, and fund-raising ideas such as the acquisition of cycle rollers, which served the dual role of charging the public to compete for the best recorded time on the one hand, and to act as bait for new membership on the other. In any event the carnival of 1978 saw a 100 per cent increase in profits over the previous year.

Autumn YH Break, 1978

Eleven club members started out on the half-term sojourn to the Kent coast during late October/early November, which broke new ground with the inclusion of a visit to both Canterbury and Dover youth hostels. Led again by Brian, the personnel for the tour was made up this time from party faithfuls Tim Cross, Adam Winter, Kane Mayhook, Matthew Gray and Jason Bonner, and included a few newer faces, namely Robin Mazinke, Gary Morley, Andy Rankin, Steve Pennells and, for a second time, Andy Bunce. From their stay at the Canterbury hostel on the first night, the group went on to Dover via Margate, visiting the miniature railway – the Romney, Hythe & Dymchurch – and, indeed, any destination that might produce a transport theme.

Folkestone was perhaps the most memorable outing of the tour for Brian who, in his relentless drive to boost club coffers, tried his hand at the 'penny falls' machine in one of the sea-front amusement arcades. By the day's end he'd accrued a deposit-account-busting 158p – a success not since repeated by him in the National Lottery – and the coining of the nickname 'mean Brian', perhaps a consequence of his unwillingness to share the winnings with the party there and then. The group did have the last laugh, however, when the arcade attendant refused to relieve Brian of the loose change that might have afforded him a more upright cycle posture for the return journey to Dover.

Dover had two hostels, one in the town centre (the Dover Town hostel) and another known as Dover Central. By elimination, the group eventually found the one for which they had been booked and the next couple of days saw them on a trip to Hythe and also to Pluckley – another village renowned for its paranormal activity.

The year finished up on something of a low as far as fundraising was concerned, with only £3 being taken at the St Mary's Church Christmas Fayre (well, it was the 'winter of discontent' for all, wasn't it?), and perhaps on a lower note still by way of repetition of the Christmas party-cum-leftovers clear-up do held at Brian's on 28 December to which 16 made it comfortably, at least for the inward part of the evening.

Additional Personnel to End of 1978

Raymond and Derek Poll, Daniel and Michael Worth, Laurence Gerrish, Sean Lewis, David Pearson, Phil Brown, Stephen Clarke, Andrew Bebbington, Simon Edgington, Michael Kruschel, Daryl Self, Gaynor Covington, Billie Mayhook, Peter Collier, Francis Muir, James Sewell, Philip Buttner, David Miller, Guy Middleton, Andrew Rankin, Stuart Masters, Jonathan Captain, Adrian Pearce, Andrew Burge, Geoff Gardiner, Mark Rutherford, Paul Gowing, Cyril Bonner, Clive Robinson, Martin James and Glenn Hurren.

1979: Dwindling Attendance and Leaderless YH Touring

Attendance during the period January to April 1979 saw a weekly average of only 17, and what began to look like a distinct downward trend. There was also a minor change in shift pattern at Brian's workplace, with the consequence that several weekend rides had to be cancelled either because of this or else due to poor winter weather.

Club morale was quickly restored, however, during the weekend of 2–4 March, which saw the first YH outing of the year to Crockham Hill and Goudhurst and was led by little-recognised club deputy Jeremy Gurton. Making up the numbers were Tim Cross, Matthew and Joanna Gray, Louise Wilson, Paul Gowing and Nick Rowe. The trip concluded satisfactorily, even if ride destinations had been short on mileage and imagination.

A further trip to the Guestling/Beachy Head hostels was arranged for the Easter Holiday period covering 17–21 April.

Seventh Petts Wood Company Girl Guides Cyclists' Badge-Testing

The spring of 1979 saw an opportunity for public service when Brian was approached by local Girl Guide leader Elizabeth Chappell to act as a tester of cycle competence for the Guides in her company (the Seventh Petts Wood) – in short, Brian was asked to arrange and provide instructions for the completion of a simple task in which the use of a bicycle would be required, and then to award a Cyclists' Badge accordingly.

In particular, the task entailed the Guide having to list three recently completed local cycle rides, noting the destinations, dates and mileages of each, and a description of the bicycle, along with a signed declaration that she would be prepared to make use of the bike in the event of an emergency, and then actually to use it during the course of delivering a prearranged message. The latter worked as follows: Brian would impart a verbal message and then instruct the Guide to cycle to a public telephone box (at a distance of about a mile away), then telephone Brian and relay the message back to him. The message would always be an authentic one, based upon factual information, and, as a help, would invariably include the Guide's own street address number. However, the temptation to introduce a transport theme into the proceedings would again prove too much, so that a typical message might read: 'The number ten bus runs from Victoria to Abridge' – the sort of information, in fact, that every ten- to fourteen-year-old should commit to memory for recall in later life!

There is no doubt that the project was a success and a useful one at that; it was particularly satisfying for Brian that his club's services should be called upon to assist in community matters. Figure 18 shows the endorsement of typical Cyclists' Badge testing documentation.

Records of the 3 cycle rides

date	The place of interest visited	miles
24th April	Chislehurst caves	6.7
20th April	Keston ponds	9.2
14th April	High Elms Ice well	9.0

1. My bicycle is a Viudec Atlantic, blue + silver its serial number is 15002~~mod~~ # and I would use it in an emergency.

Geraldine Duncan.

passed guides Cyclist badge 29/4/79

Figure 18 Girl Guides' Cyclist Badge paperwork

The BHF London-to-Brighton Charity Event

On 12 May the club had their annual London-to-Brighton jaunt for the British Heart Foundation charity fund-raiser. Had the party set out to Brighton from Green Street Green, each member would have had to cycle a minimum of 120 miles, which would have limited the number of hours that could be spent pleasurably at the event. Instead, the group cycled to BR Bromley South (having first waited in vain for over an hour for the Orpington to Charing Cross), alighted in London, and then completed the short ride to the journey's starting-point at Marble Arch.

From Brighton, the club took the train to East Croydon and completed the journey's remainder by bike.

The Rabbits Farm Incident, June 1979

Not unlike the calamity which had befallen the club during 'Black sunday' back in May 1976, the upset that became known as The Rabbits Farm Incident had started equally innocently, as a ride to Upnor Castle. About an hour into the ride, on Rabbits Road between Horton Kirby and Longfield, the congestion that inevitably built as the party of nine snaked through the twisting country lanes caused an impatient (local) driver of a dark-coloured saloon (so specific is Brian's memory) to become boxed in amongst them. Ever eager to save a precious second or two, the engine-revving owner of the car hastily swung towards the offside of the road and, in doing so, it was alleged he deliberately flung open the driver's door, sending member number 274, Kevin Rowe, into the hedgerow at considerable speed. Kevin was quickly taken to West Hill hospital, along with brother Nick, Brian and Andy Turrell (271), who each went on to make statements to the Dartford police. As it happened, the driver of the car was not even cautioned for driving without due care and attention. In the meantime, the show continued, with Jeremy leading the remaining party of five to Chatham.

The Curse of the Borley Brickwork?

Altogether, 1979 was proving to be an epitome of disaster for the club in terms of the infrequency of rides and what was happening during some of them, and also because of the subdued activity in general. The next 'incident' occurred on the way to Ardingly Showground in Sussex, site of an annual Steam Rally - an event for which the admission charged to each member would be subsidised from club funds. In any event, it was Keith Howkins (number 55) who, riding a poorly maintained Peugeot, suffered a sudden back tyre blow-out near Turner's Hill, forcing him to complete the remaining five miles on a flat tyre and, by then, buckled wheel (despite many a vain roadside attempt to repair the recalcitrant inner tube). Fortune would have it that one of Brian's workmates, Fred Chapman, was also attending the rally in one of Bromley Garage Motor Club's old single-decker RF London buses. He kindly agreed to ferry Keith and his defunct metal home again afterwards. Had Mr Howkins' Peugeot *really* suffered a genuine, accidental, flat or had it been another of Brian's convoluted engineerings to convince his doubting work colleagues that Green Street Green Cycling Club did exist, and that they would have to believe him now? For sure, we'll never know.

YH Extravaganza, 1979

The latter part of 1979 saw a quickfire succession of YH trips (in fact, almost as though lost time was being made up for), with a summer holiday venture to Colchester/Nedging Tye and the first in a series of evening rides (this one to the local village, Fingringhoe) that would set a trend in pub visits for those old enough to drink. The tour casualty list ran to three this time: Robin Mazinke slipped off his bike while showing off in a ford near Ipswich (where was his Escort?); Fiona suffering something of a decidedly feminine nature; while Steve Nunn developed that ever useful stand-by, 24-hour flu. Robin can be seen in Figure 19, definitely

Figure 19 Robin Mazinke, 1979

up to no good, only hours before his downfall.

From 21–23 September the Club (led by Jeremy) went on a weekend tour of Kemsing and Blackboys hostels. The party comprised club regulars Tim Cross, Matthew and Joanna, Robin, Louise and Fiona; and also Green Street Green's second Asian member, Arif Khan who remained with the club until October 1980. (The very first Asian participation in the club was way back in 1973 with the fleeting membership of local resident Gurmeet Jaggee.)

A final tour for 1979 took a party of six, fronted by Jeremy, to local hostels Crockham Hill and Ewhurst Green during late November.

Additional Personnel to End of 1979

Laurence Burton, Stephen Coulson, Chris Cade, Guy Sims, Mark Oldham, Tony Docherty, Richard Stone, Neil Runham, Philip Orr, Julie Stephenson, Michael Wild, Kevin Marshall, Stephen Lee, Grant Pilcher, Richard Luff, Gary Picker, Matthew Adams, Robert Nunn, Martin Holmberg, Peter Graham, Mark Davis, Chris Bush, John Dalton, Martin Troubridge, Mark Lettington, David Collett, Mark Hussey, Ian Lohse, Robert Morgan, Clive Hogan, David Harris, Andrew Hyde and Robert Tomlinson.

7

The Pinnacle Year, 1980

Introduction to 1980

Brian describes 1980 as a particularly adventurous year for Green Street Green Cycling Club. It was a year in which the 'big' YH pilgrimage to Devon and Cornwall took place and in which both he and Jeremy set about designing and building the club's own trailer specifically for the transporting of their bikes. It was also the year in which the club received local recognition by means of a special grant awarded by Bromley council; in which club attendance would once again attain the levels of the mid-1970s, and which would also see the launch of the club's own magazine, *Green Wheels,* an informative and amusing periodical edited by brother-and-sister team members Matthew and Jo Gray. The place to begin a look at 1980, however, would have to be with the home-construction of the club trailer in preparation for the Devon and Cornwall YH venture.

The Club Trailer Sponsored Ride

Funds to help buy materials for the trailer (cycle transporter) were amassed via the sponsored ride scheduled for 24 February and then rescheduled for the 28th due to poor weather, in which 16 participated. The cycle route (shown in Figure 20) begins at Starts Hill Road, takes the second left turning into Lovibonds Avenue, passes Mada and Mosslea Roads and Highwood Drive, turning left again, into

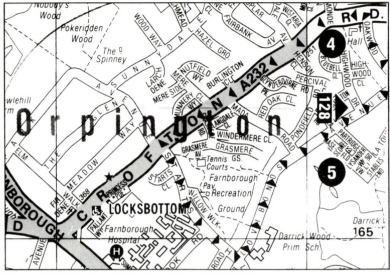

Figure 20   Sponsored ride (for club trailer), 1980

Oakwood Road, and then takes a further left onto (the A232) Crofton Road, finishing at the beginning at Starts Hill Road again. Each circuit constitutes a lap of 1½ miles. The total raised was £50 which, put together with the £35 grant from Bromley council and the Green Street Green Summer Fête takings of £45, made a total of £130.

The club's decision to build a trailer rather than 'buy off the peg' was made for three reasons: firstly, to cut expenditure to about half; secondly, to stimulate club activity and sense of achievement by building something from scratch and thirdly, and equally important, to construct a trailer of sufficient capacity to ensure the carriage of the dozen or so bikes it was envisaged would need transporting. Having looked at the possibility of buying from a specialist and finding nothing quite the right size – a situation not too dissimilar, perhaps, to the dilemma facing Barry White when needing a new pair of trousers – it was decided that a 'custom job' it would have to be. Dimensions of 6 ft 8 in. long by 5 ft 3 in. wide by 2 ft deep had been decided, first ensuring ease of driving access through the narrowest (6 ft 6 in.) width restriction.

The next job was to set about obtaining the construction materials, namely angle-irons, hubs, suspension, mudguards and coupling, plywood for the sides and floorings, lighting board and registration number-plate, flat steel strips, two tyres (eventually sourced from an Austin Mini and then a spare from a scrapyard), along with tubs of priming paint, undercoat and black gloss and, lastly, creosote for application to the floorings and trailer payload areas.

Now, because his taste is his own, Brian favoured for the trailer's livery a particularly bright, almost fluorescent, shade of green known as 'Monte Carlo', proposing this would suit the club's identity i.e. Green Street Green. A valid point, but with mutterings of 'environmental friendliness' – a buzz-word not even coined by 1980 – this rationale would have to be dis-

Figure 21 Sharing a joke: Devon and Cornwall tour, Summer 1980

missed. If nothing else, the trailer would prove visible to every motorist for miles and is believed to be the single most important factor in the trailer having never been accident-damaged throughout its eight-year period of ownership.

The actual construction of the transporter took only a few weeks. The chassis was laid on Jeremy's driveway at his house in Chislehurst Road, assisted by little more than an electric arc welder and a background in O-level metalwork. Independent suspension was sourced from a specialist firm in Shirley. In all, the trailer (which hadn't yet been assigned a club membership number) had cost the best part of £150, and £100 of that was recovered upon selling to a specialist trailer firm later in 1989.

With Project Trailer out of the way, then, things began to look up. The club would now be able to travel to youth hostels and visit sights, thereby breaking free from the restrictions of having to use the same hostel circuit, a pattern itself fashioned by the maximum distance that could be comfortably cycled by the club in a single day.

The hostels chosen for the tour (Figure 21) included the southern Cornish site of Golant in Fowey (pronounced 'foy'), which would serve as both start and finish points for the tour, in addition to being a suitable site for the trailer's storage. Moving on to Pendennis Castle (part-castle, part-hostel), the party would cross over to the more northerly hostels of Hayle, Newquay and Boscastle, and then on to Tavistock, before finally returning to Golant to undertake the return journey by road back to Orpington.

Devon and Cornwall: The First Setback

The party of nine, which included Brian's wife Renie, set out on the morning of 27 July in two cars: Brian's trusty (although also rather rusty) Austin 1100, housing Matthew, Robin, Andy Turrell and Renie, and also Jeremy's tasteful and restrained 1973 MKI canary-yellow Capri, into which had been shoehorned Jo, Louise and Garry Morris. The only minor aberrations from what was an otherwise uneventful motorway cruise were the excessive speed to which the trailer was put (80 m.p.h.) and the deviation from the route at the A38 turn-off, resulting in Jeremy and his group of three heading for Plymouth. When the red-faced quartet did make it to the hostel, it was with a limping trailer down on its offside rear on account of having come undone, causing the eight bikes to list in sympathy. During the week of cycling, the hostel warden kindly arranged for a one-man welding outfit to come and repair the trailer, adding a tenner's worth of extra supporting cross-members to the structure.

The Second 'Event'

It was somewhere between Newquay and Boscastle, while descending a steep hill which veered suddenly into a rather tight right-hand bend, that both Jeremy and Garry Morris collided, careering into a wall of flint. This resulted in multiple cuts and abrasions in addition to two written-off cycles. It also saw Garry cutting short his holiday and departing the group the very next day via Bodmin Road train station (and an unscheduled return to Golant by Jeremy to collect the corroding Capri in which to do this). The accident, too, left Jeremy without a serviceable bike, although this was not entirely without its compensations since he'd just discovered girls – and particularly Louise, who proved willing to forsake the cycling part of her holiday in order to explore the West Country by car with Jeremy. As if through duty, the two would turn up at the hostel to meet the remainder of the group, down to only five now.

A Close Thing

The remainder of the tour was progressing satisfactorily, despite the temporary loss of some key personnel, although it was also true that the daytime outings had sapped the group's appetite for all nocturnal cycle activity. As mentioned above, the group was now down to five, and it was on a particular evening during this time that Brian decided on a solo hike

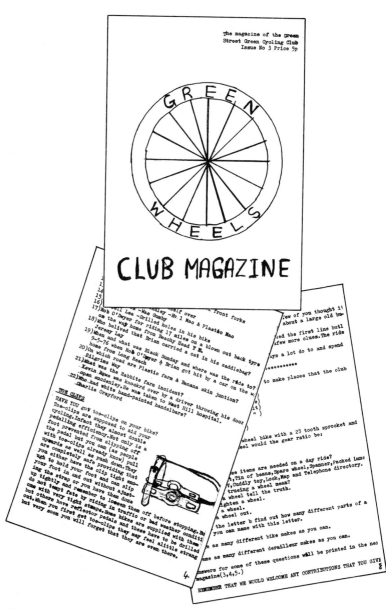

Figure 22 *Green Wheels* magazine, 1980

along the nearby and, needless to say, disused stretch of the Tavistock-to-Plymouth railway line. Brian recalls entering the Shillamill Tunnel, and in particular that he actually *counted* the 673 yards of 'pitch-black' before deciding to about face and make back for the hostel. With a club leader able to come up with facts and figures as inspiring as this, who knows if it was the right thing to allow Brian to come back; the club might have developed a quite different persona had the nucleus of four back in the dormitory had the wherewithal to effect the necessary changes.

Green Wheels – The Unofficial Green Street Green Cycling Club Magazine

It was during 1980, too, that Matthew and Jo Gray took it upon themselves to produce a Green Street Green Cycling Club magazine for and on behalf of club members. The magazine, an irregular, even sporadic, publication, was a delightfully amateur affair, although perhaps this was a strength. Comprising a dozen or so yellowing sheets of badly trimmed A5, the undated magazine cover depicted the club's motif – a one-dimensional bicycle wheel with radial spokes – which would find itself stapled to the other pages making up the booklet (Figure 22). It was the magazine's content, however, that best illustrated the commitment and depth of feeling the club generated amongst its following during these peak years. Invariably, each issue would begin with a round-up of the previous quarter's events, including a review of, say, a recent London-to-Brighton outing, official club statistics (including club attendance figures), ride capacities, a club members' survey, in addition to mini-quizzes of a cycling or general nature. Jokes, illustrations, cyclo-cross routes and other club trivia were also particularly well represented.

Green Wheels had a serious role, too, in detailing Club fund-raising and listing forthcoming YH attractions; and there would be informative and interesting articles on, for example, 'How to Get More from Your Cycling' or 'The Importance of Cycle Toe-Clips' and 'The Advantages and

Disadvantages of Fitting Your Bike with Mudguards'.

There was once a crossword included, the point about it being its complete irrelevance to all matters cycling! And how about this for the last word in suspense: a three-part mystery thriller entitled *The Holiday*, in which a group of four cyclists arrange a youth hostel trip to the south coast and meet with punctures, flooding, blackmail and even the kidnap of one of their members. Introduced in Issue No. 2, the story continues into No. 3, therein promising to deliver the final part, which fails to materialise!

The magazine also, in its relatively short run, produced a brace of budding poets. Regrettably, there is insufficient room for inclusion of such epics as editor-in-chief Matthew Gray's *A Knackering Ride*, or *Sarah's Custard*, or indeed Robin Mazinke's village-renowned *Steak & Kidney Pie*. However, there surely cannot be many seasoned club cyclists who would find difficulty relating to Mr Gray's Smash, a well-observed tribute to the famous brand of instant mashed potato served up by Brian at what would seem to be every meal – sweet or savoury. In this work, Matthew introduces us to the verb 'to luzz', meaning 'to spoon out unceremoniously'.

SMASH
Smash is a horrible runny white, it makes you sick at
every sight,
Brian prepares it in a pot, where it enters the plate
looking like slop,
It is then luzzed upon a plate, making you wonder if
you've met your fate,
Your thoughts turn then to the dustbin, and all the smash
shortly goes therein,
Brian tries hard to eat his smash,
But when everyone has gone he, too, luzzes it in the bin
marked 'trash'.

Only a true philistine could fail to appreciate the Booker Prize-winning potential in *Smash*, and the likes of *Beans* and *Steak & Kidney Pie*.

The Rest of the Year

In fact, 1980 kicked off with a brand new ride, in January, to a place called Holly Hill, Dode. By now several club members had become accustomed to the 'theme rides' which would often as not climax with a visit to a defunct or disused railway line or haunted building, and so the church at Holly Hill was no exception. The ride had even been suggested by a club member who had heard or read somewhere that the church had not seen service since about the fourteenth century on account of a one-time plague (the Black Death) that had befallen the village. Still in 1980, entry to the church-yard was prevented by a reinforced barbed wire enclosure as if to emphasise the severity of dangers past. The site, too, took a particular determination to reach on the part of the group, involving the traversing of sodden muddy tracks and obscure footpaths, which in turn gave several members' bikes minor punctures that had to be repaired throughout the persistent drizzle.

Gatwick Airport

The trip to Gatwick Airport, not a new ride by any means and in fact one of the more frequented of club destinations, warrants a mention here, perhaps because of its very unlikeliness as the end point of a club ride. The route chosen for 19 February was a particularly green and scenic one, commencing from Green Street Green and taking the party up through Cudham Lane, Grays Road and Westerham, and riding into Edenbridge, through Dormansland and Lingfield then on to Felbridge, via Newchapel. Country and minor roads were used where practicable and, from here, the B2028 was selected as the route to Effingham Park (considered a one-time cycle destination in its own right); then onto the B2037 just north of Copthorne, over the Black Corner stretch of the M23 to Tinsley Green and along the A23 all the way to, and then just past, the cargo area, where the group would park their bikes at the then Gatwick Station. After downing a packed lunch of sandwiches and cartoned drinks in the familiar bus shelter that had over the years become a makeshift cafeteria for the club, there was a visit to the spectators' viewing gallery for an hour or three of off-the-record planespotting – weren't they the days!

Other outings for the 1980 season took in the annual visit to Kew Gardens in May, and also Box Hill in Surrey; Aylesford, Toad Rock in Tunbridge Wells, Yalding, Southend, Hever and Knole.

Two Mini-Tours For 1980

There were two further mini-YH tours in 1980, including one that was very nearly cancelled. One, in November, took a party of just three: Matthew, Robin and Andy Turrell, who between them organised a weekend in and around Crockham Hill and Doddington. Another, very much earlier in the year, covered the period 11–14 April, with only Brian and Jason Bonner planning to go to the Sussex hostel at Arundel over the Easter period. Not that this would have been an unpopular trip by any means, only that many had pre-booked and were saving themselves for the 'big' Devon and Cornwall venture in the summer.

Right at the last moment, however, Jason pulled out, leaving Brian with an already paid-for club tour itinerary but with no one to share it. With only 36 hours to go, he was on the verge of cancelling the trip, until a chance meeting with club member 185, Phil Turner, who quite happily agreed to a few days' cycling in the fresh air, particularly if his being called upon meant helping to prevent an aborted tour.

Though he wouldn't go as far as awarding even a single extra 'mileage point', Brian recalls being especially appreciative of this type of commitment shown by another member to the club and at such short notice, mentioning retrospectively that it had added to an already significant year in the club's 20-year history. In any event, Brian was able to look back over the year as another important milestone, enabling subsequent club YH tours to take place in areas of the country previously forbidden by distance (and already a second 'big' tour was earmarked for Oxfordshire and Worcester for 1981). It was also a time during which several prominent Green Street Green members organised club as well as solo YH party ventures and, in the process, helped to take some of the responsibility from Brian's previously overburdened shoulders.

Additional Personnel to End of 1980

Jonathan Scully, Simon Street, Mark Cluer, Matt Watson, Paul Lambourne, Beverley Smith, David Cakebread, Vincent Lamb, Simon Castle, John Penfold, David Alchin, Ralph Beddall, David Wetz, Steven and Richard Breach, Martin Eva, Michael Paul, Marco and Lee Goldsmith, Kevin Smith, John Willis, Jonathan Guy, Chris Wilson and David Harrison.

8

1981 – The Club's Heyday

Building New Rides on Past Strengths

The year 1981 began in much the same way that 1980 had left off, seeing the club in good fettle, completing a series of ambitious – as well as fairly effortless – YH tours, and ready support for many of the organisational tasks coming from a nucleus of key club members. The lengthening list of cycle outings now at the club's disposal, and the keenness with which the members wanted to participate, indeed marked this period in the history of Green Street Green Cycling Club as something of a golden age.

All the old favourite routes were trotted out in easy succession, and included, among the highlights, rides to Gravesend, Tonbridge and Longfield, Tunbridge Wells, Gatwick Airport, Maidstone and Hampton Court; Whipps Cross, Edenbridge and the fairly recent destination of Earlswood Lakes situated just south of Redhill. Earlswood Lakes was a particular winter favourite, proving popular with many riders if only for the challenge of traversing the 'mud bath' track leading to Earlswood's central feature, a boating lake-cum-paddling pool most often used for racing tournaments involving small remote-controlled boats. During winter, though, much fun could be had by the members arriving at the lake and smashing its dense frozen crust into smaller, indivisible blocks – such was the progressive nature of a club having a collective IQ well into double figures.

YH Tour, Easter 1981

April 1981 saw the first YH outing of the year, which was arranged for Arundel again, although this time the tour party comprised a mainly newer membership and one which would herald the beginnings of a new era. Gone were club stalwarts Matthew and Jo Gray, Jeremy Gurton, Louise Wilson, Andy Turrell, Andrew Bunce and Garry Morris, and in were Gareth Howells, Olly Reed, David Rumm, Andy Braben and James Malzer. In, too, was Shaun Dooley, Brian's foster-son, who was to remain with the club for the duration of the 1980–81 cycling season. Ride destinations during the Arundel three-nighter took in the coastal resorts of Littlehampton, Brighton, Bognor Regis and both East and West Witterings. Of particular note was the accompaniment of racing enthusiast and recent club adjunct Derek 'Del Boy' Taylor, who not only travelled with the club all the way to Arundel, but back again to Orpington in the same day. Now whether Derek caught a train back part of the way or, indeed, whether he cycled the full 120 - plus miles, it is clear the man needed locking up! Derek became an influential member of the club's latter years and went on to win the Green Street Green President's Cup in successive seasons spanning summer 1982 to winter 1984, and then again in the summer of 1988, after which the Cup was discontinued.

The London-to-Brighton

May 1981 witnessed the largest ever club turn-out for the London-to-Brighton British Heart Foundation charity run with a high of 24. The trip included a complement of four visiting members, including Phil Gray (Matthew and Jo's father) and a friend of Steve Pennells'. That this was a most pleasant trip and featured excellent weather throughout, would have to go down as another of the high points in club history.

Summer YH Tour: Colchester, Nedging Tye, 1981

This, the second YH venture of the year saw a line-up of Brian, Olly Reed, Phil Turner, Andy Braben and Shaun Dooley on a tour around East Anglia, the beginnings of some tension within the club and a modification of the way in which it would conduct some of its inter-hostel excursions.

The group of five set out from Worlds End Lane by car to Suffolk, with plans to deposit the trailer in the hostel grounds of Nedging Tye. The car used by Brian at the time was his old Austin 1100, a banger known affectionately as 'Wreckage' on account of its ageing 1968 bodywork – a car old even at first manufacture – and registration letter grouping 'RKJ' (see the list of popular Loakesisms in Appendix II). They arrived shortly after midday, and the first ride of the tour was scheduled for the old nineteenth-century wool town of Lavenham, five or so miles north of Sudbury, and home to the beautiful old Guildhall, an historic building whose virtues were probably lost on all present but Brian. That day, 14 August, also took in an evening trip to nearby Kersey, renowned by previous club generations for its heavily duck-populated ford and also its local pub, which was indulged in by all this time. The ensuing tour dates saw a round of trips that encompassed the Felixstowe and Clacton destination regulars, prior to moving on for the party's single-night booking at Colchester YH, and then the return to Nedging Tye to collect the trailer.

The source of much of the friction that developed during the tour had had to do with a clash of personality between the somewhat unruly Shaun Dooley and the more reserved, private school-educated Andy Braben, who, like the rest of us, perhaps never really made an early connection between his continually flat (tyre) inner tubes and the menacing omnipresence of Shaun and his collection of sharp tools. Brian's reticence in dealing with a situation that ought to have been nipped in the bud, and one which could have started to sour the atmosphere as a whole, resulted in Phil leading Shaun and Andy by a more direct route to Colchester, while Brian and Olly took a more prolonged excursion via Flatford Mill.

A Continuing Success

A good fund-raising bank holiday at the Norman Park Bromley Carnival (£60), for which there had been a good show of membership, was followed in September by the enrolment of four new members at the Keston Scout Hut: including the Haylock brothers, Mark and Peter (numbers 363 and 364), from nearby Ravensbourne school and Jerry Adams (number 362) also from Ravensbourne. Early October, too, had seen introduction of the first West Indian addition to the cycling club, one Lawrence Webb (number 365) from Hayes Lane. Like Shaun, in that he was thought to have been adopted, Lawrence sported a brown-coloured American Huffy racer upon which Brian had commented on its unusual bottom bracket/crank assembly; the cranks themselves apparently were of round instead of oval section. Lawrence did not attend many outings though he had stayed with the club for the remainder of the 1981-82 season.

The 'Nine Counties' YH Tour, October 1981

The club had been set on another trip to East Anglia, a popular choice, due in no small part to the abundance of flat roads and pleasant landscape, much of it farmland that could be seen for miles. However, because of an internal rationalisation within the YHA (Youth Hostels Association), Nedging Tye had had to be closed down, which led the group to thinking once more about a cycling venture in a whole new part of the country. Various tour venues were considered (the hostel standard and distance between each being the limiting criteria), and in the end Oxford, Stratford-upon-Avon in Warwickshire, old Northampton favourite Badby, and Ivinghoe on the Hertfordshire-Bedfordshire border were selected for a tour that would take the group through nine different counties (in 1982, this would be surpassed by the 'ten counties' tour), making a pleasant circular trip with only moderate travelling distances between each of the four chosen stopping-points. The nine counties traversed were, in geographical order: Kent, London/Middlesex, Buckinghamshire, Oxfordshire, Warwickshire, Worcestershire, Northampton and Hertfordshire.

Green Street Green to Oxford proved, of course, to be a challenging 85 miles and was completed by participants Brian, Gareth Howells, Olly Reed, David Rumm and Shaun Dooley. As a club detour, the party visited Worcester town and cathedral. The only minor departure from the route laid down occurred between Badby and Ivinghoe youth hostels along a stretch of the A421, where Brian spied a section of hedgerow full of mostly ripe, unpicked blackberries which would be unlikely to survive the few weeks now prior to the onset of winter. Of course, this scenario was rather like a red rag to a bull where Brian was concerned, and he insisted upon the whole lot being picked and either eaten or stored there and then, with even the unripe green ones finding their way into Brian's saddlebag. Even then, the misdemeanour was only brought to a conclusion when a dutiful policeman was sent in to ease the escalating traffic congestion by asking the blackberry-stained five to move on.

The return journey from Ivinghoe to Elstree was pleasant enough, the only part of it able to mar the trip was the messy Elstree-to-home stretch along the Edgware Road, continuing through Cricklewood, Maida Vale and into central London via Marble Arch, Hyde Park and Victoria. The heavy traffic only really clearing by the time the party had made it to Forest Hill, before the final home stretch through Catford and then Bromley.,

The end-of-year highlight was, of course, the Worlds End Lane Christmas do on 29 December, which 12 attended, to engage in all manner of club-related tittle-tattle.

Additional Personnel to End of 1981

Justin Pitman, Jeremy Melluish, Paul Frankland, Warren Haines, Graham Barnes, Michael Jones, Michael Yarwood, Suzanne Marlow, Tom Wood, Stephen Ranson, Jonathan Todd, Simon Devese, Maurice Wells, Stephen and Philip Sewell, Martin Alden, Chris Wilkinson, Ray Gearing, Adam Crombie, Paula Hackett, David Kirk, Grant Weall and Ian Badis.

9

Ten Years of The Green Street Green Cycling Club, 1982–83

A Slightly Downward Trend

Although the beginning of each new club year could show a slow start, this would usually be explained by the inclement winter weather in conjunction with an adjustment by much of the active membership toward a new school term following the Christmas and New Year festivities. But whereas the weekly club night attendance figures for the 1980–81 seasons had been in the order of 12 to 15, the Thursday night turnouts during this corresponding period did not attain even double figures, a trend which persisted more or less until August 1982. There was, too, the inevitable hand-in-hand relationship between the weekly club night turnout and the numbers making it to the Sunday/evening rides. That this was noted sufficiently early by both Brian and a few other key members helped give a rebirth to some sorely missed club activities, and add some others which were quite new. Meanwhile, enthusiasm for YH touring continued unabated, and two such tours were arranged that year, including Arundel in Sussex during Easter, and also the Ten Counties tour of the south Midlands in October. Both trips were well-attended.

A New Vigour For 1982

The first of the new activities saw a link-up with the Catford CC, who traditionally held their annual 'Reliability Ride' on the last Sunday in January, which entailed a 65-mile round cycling trip commencing at the Rose & Crown roundabout at Green Street Green. Four Green Street Green Club members took part, namely Olly Reed, Gareth Howells and racing merchants David Rumm and Derek Taylor, the latter propinquity bringing the club at least a degree of kudos by managing to finish the course! Such a success was the event that it was repeated in January 1983, with three victors this time: Gareth Howells, Derek Taylor and Simon Long.

Return of the Time-Trial

After completion of the Sussex YH trip during Easter, which had taken in the now familiar tour destinations of Brighton, Bognor and the Witterings, and also the annual London-to-Brighton day trip in May, summer brought about a renewed interest in time-trialling. Much of the impetus for these events originated from Messrs Taylor, Rumm and Montaldo, with the weekday races themselves attended by a further handful of budding Phil Andersons and Greg Lemondes, namely Martin Baker, Gareth Howells and Oliver Reed, the latter allegedly on a filming break.

Marsh Green, Edenbridge

The ride to Marsh Green, just south of Edenbridge, deserves especial mention if only, perhaps, because it was one of those rare outings (rather like the later one-off to North Woolwich) recorded in the club diary as being on the way to somewhere else that became the ride's end-point due to the onset of bad weather. In this particular instance, one of the more timid party member's bikes found its way lodged intimately within the upper framework of a slide within a childrens' playground. Upon the arrival of the park orderly, there ensued a heavy silence lasting at least a minute before he addressed the grinning 'hooligans' with the dry rhetoric (and from then on, often-repeated club expression): '*I suppose you think that's funny...*' Rides taking the club to and around Edenbridge would never be quite the same again.

In a further bid to revive faltering club attendance, Brian began awarding mileage points to existing members upon the successful recruitment of newer ones managing to attend a total of three club nights and/or rides within their first four consecutive weeks. For this, the recruiting member would receive three points, although it had been very much a trend in recent years for several new cyclists to join the club of their own accord. On 9 September, then, there was an influx of three interested parties from local schools and, in the following week, a further three turned up at the Keston Scout hut, all from Ravensbourne school – one being Mark Young from West Wickham, who claimed to have seen an old poster detailing the club's activities, which had prompted him to write a letter of introduction (now who says that advertising doesn't pay?). An assortment of advertisements and posters devised by Green Street Green Cycling Club can be seen in Figure 23.

The Club's Tenth Anniversary Reunion

From as early as the Easter holiday in 1982, there were plans afoot to mark the club's tenth anniversary with a reunion that would bring together members past and present and, in June, a tentative letter was mailed to each, offering a size of buffet-type meal according to the numbers that would attend. Originally, the church hall at St Mary's in Worlds End Lane had been a preferred venue before considering the authenticity of using the present Keston site Certainly, St Mary's would have afforded better car-parking facilities for the hordes of past members envisaged to be attending, but then perhaps Brian had decided that the restricted parking in the few culs-de-sac situated off the Croydon Road would persuade more of the partygoers to arrive by bike. How naive!

The format of the reunion, it was decided, would be a 'nosh and natter' affair and would take place on 18 September, very nearly ten years to the exact date of the Club's inception and, fortuitously, falling on a Saturday evening; so it was hoped

Figure 23 Some of the posters, ads and general publicity used by Green Street Green Cycling Club to attract new members

GREEN ST GREEN CYCLING CLUB

THE GREEN ST. GREEN CYCLING CLUB WELCOMES ALL YOUNG CYCLISTS EVERY THURSDAY EVENING
7 - 9 pm AT The Saxon Centre, Lychgate Road,
~~THE SCOUT GROUP HEADQUARTERS~~ ORPINGTON
EVENING ACTIVITIES INCLUDE TABLE TENNIS, DARTS, RECORDS, REFRESHMENTS ETC.,
PLUS RIDES AT WEEKENDS AND IN THE SCHOOL HOLIDAYS .. TIME TRIALS .. YOUTH HOSTELLING
FURTHER DETAILS ARE AVAILABLE FROM THE CLUB LEADER
BRIAN LOAKES, 52 WORLDS END LANE, ORPINGTON. TEL: 66 54414.
....
POSTER   POSTER   PLEASE DISPLAY IN YOUR CLUB   POSTER   POSTER

GREEN ST GREEN CYCLING CLUB

THE GREEN ST. GREEN CYCLING CLUB WELCOMES ALL YOUNG CYCLISTS EVERY THURSDAY EVENING AT
THE SCOUT HUT, 143 CROYDON ROAD, KESTON FROM 6.30 PM ONWARDS

EVENING ACTIVITIES INCLUDE TABLE TENNIS, DARTS, RECORDS, REFRESHMENTS ETC.,
PLUS RIDES AT WEEKENDS AND IN THE SCHOOL HOLIDAYS .. TIME TRIALS .. YOUTH HOSTELLING

FURTHER DETAILS ARE AVAILABLE FROM THE CLUB LEADER
BRIAN LOAKES, 52 WORLDS END LANE, ORPINGTON. TEL: 66 54414.

that excuses for inability to attend would be kept to a bare minimum. Figure 24 shows a sample reunion ticket along with a handful of replies to the invitation.

The Ten Per Cent Club

Now whether the slightly disappointing turnout of only 34 was due, at least in part, to Brian having set a ticket admission price of £1 (though equally harrowing was the distinct possibility that he might use the event to try to recover all unpaid subs since 1975), or whether potential attendees realised intuitively that 'nosh and natter' would probably mean having to bring one's own food, we cannot be sure. However, if we consider the numbers that had possibly moved away from the area and could not therefore be contacted easily at such relatively short notice, then perhaps the gathering of around 10 per cent was not so calamitous after all – and particularly considering that just over one-third of those present were members joining prior to 1973.

```
                    GREEN  STREET  GREEN  CYCLING  CLUB

                                                52 World's End Lane,
                                                Green Street Green,
Farnborough 54414                               Orpington. BR6 6AG.


                                                16th June, 1982.


Dear

     We are contacting former members of the Club to see if you would
be interested in taking part in a kind of reunion at St. Mary's Hall,
World's End Lane (subject to availability) on Saturday,
18th September, 1982 to commemorate the tenth anniversary of our
foundation.

     The form that this would take will obviously depend on the
numbers attending.  It is likely that a buffet type meal would be best
for the occasion, but any ideas or comments you may have would be most
welcome.  So that details and cost can be worked out, would you please
complete and return the portion below as soon as possible.  Even if
you are not interested, it would be nice to hear from you anyway.

                         Yours truly,


                         Brian Loakes


P.S.  If replying before 29th June, please contact Keith Howkins,
      125 Park Avenue, Orpington.  (Orp. 23793)



.....................................................................

I have received your letter.  Please send me further details.
(Friends, wives, husbands would be most welcome).
```

Myself	
Wife	
Husband	
Girl-Friend	
Boy-Friend	

```
Signed
      ........................

Address (if different from
when joining Club):-
```

Please tick

Figure 24   Ten-year anniversary 'natter and nosh' do, 1982 (tickets, replies, newspaper publicity/cuttings etc)

23 Sevenoaks Road,
Orpington,
Kent.
20th July 1982

Dear Mr Loakes,

We were surprised and pleased to see your invitation to Stewart to attend your tenth anniversary reunion.

Unfortunately, it is very unlikely that Stewart would be able to attend, as he is now serving in Belfast with the Royal Fusiliers.

Nevertheless, we will send your invitation to him so that he may see that he has been remembered. We hope your reunion will be a great success.

Sincerely

A.M. & K. Pettet

KEN BIRD'S BICYCLE CENTRE
35/37 HIGH STREET, GREEN STREET GREEN, ORPINGTON, KENT
TELEPHONE: FARNBOROUGH (KENT) 53746

37 ANERLEY ROAD, CRYSTAL PALACE, LONDON S.E.19. 2AS
TELEPHONE: 01-778-5330

Our Ref./INVOICE No. KB1/FAS

Your Ref./INVOICE No. ....

15th September 1982

To: Mr. Brian Loakes,
    52 World's End Lane,
    GREEN STREET GREEN,
    Orpington, Kent.

Dear Brian,

    Thank you for your note and tickets regarding your 10th anniversary re-union of the GSGCC on Saturday 18th September. As already intimated, Janet and I are both delighted to accept your kind invitation and look forward to seeing you all next Saturday.

        Yours sincerely,

                      (Ken Bird)
        KEN BIRD'S BICYCLE CENTRE

KEN BIRD - 25 YEARS IN THE CYCLE TRADE 1955-1980

V.A.T. Reg. No. 206 6087 74

Registered Office : 35 HIGH STREET, GREEN STREET GREEN, ORPINGTON, KENT.
A Member of the National Association of Cycle Traders.

Orpington 35466

158 Avalon Road
Orpington
Kent
BR6 9BB

24th July 1982

Dear Brian,

Many thanks for your letter. I am pleased to hear that the club has continued successfully.

I regret that other commitments prevent me from attending the reunion, but I hope you all have a most enjoyable evening

Best wishes

CHRIS THOMPSON.

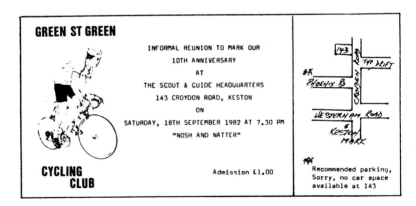

26, Tintagel Road,
Orpington,
Kent BR5 4LG

16 September 1982

Dear Brian,

Sorry for taking so long to answer your letter, I had misplaced it and so did not have your address.

Unfortunately I am unable to attend the reunion due to prior commitments though I hope it is a good evening.

As for the cycling, I must confess that for the past three years or so I have hardly pushed a pedal. This is because I am in the middle of taking a degree and so most of my time is taken up with studying.

About five years ago I tried track racing, my school was a few hundred yards from Herne Hill cycle track. I progressed to racing against other schoolboys from schools around London, with some success albeit short-lived.

Hopefully I shall begin cycling again by the middle of next year and will keep in touch.

Yours Sincerely

Gerald C. Buckle.

Cycling club

ABOUT fifty members past and present of the Green Street Green Cycling Club attended a reunion on Saturday, September 18, at the Scout HQ in Croydon Road, Keston, to celebrate the 10th Anniversary of the club.

Guest of honour was Mr Ken Bird of Ken Bird Cycles.

The club meets weekly on Thursday evenings and regular runs are arranged mostly at weekends.

The next Youth Hostel tour is during the half term holiday in October and takes in Oxford, Stratford-on-Avon and the Chilterns.

Prospective members can contact the leader Brian Loakes on Farnborough 54414.

Of course, over and above the merriment and banter there existed a hidden agenda in that it might be hoped the reunion would encourage older members to rejoin the club – at least for a few rides – or that some of the visiting contingent, invited by current club members, would be persuaded to take the plunge.

Guest of Honour

Some described it as the party without booze, others as a chance to meet those they had known previously only by name. So how did the affair go? Brian, initially a little apprehensive over the mix of existing and former membership, need not have worried much since it wasn't too long before racing enthusiast Mike Thorogood could be overheard exaggerating finishing times with more recent member Derek Taylor (both of the Syndenham Wheelers Cycling Club, incidentally, and, in passing, perhaps we ought to make mention of the fact that over the years, Green Street Green would prove to be a fairly regular recruiter of new members for the Sydenhams.

Certainly, any newcomer displaying a propensity towards racing would as often as not find himself joining the local Sydenham team before too long and, in addition to Derek Taylor and Mike Thorogood then, other former Green Street Green members to have crossed the line to the Sydenham's included among them Garry Pulling (153), Michael Franklin (388) and Peter Mahoney (458).) Neither was it very long before somebody would own up to the 'jellyfish-in-the-saddle-bag' incident at Southend in 1975; or recall that, as Sunday morning cyclists, it wouldn't be out of the ordinary to be greeted at Brian's house at 52 World's End Lane by the sound of a steam train LP being played at full blast; or else that time Brian would attempt a makeshift puncture repair by extensively padding an inner tyre wall – with handfuls of grass.

No, it wasn't too long, in fact, before the ice was well and truly broken, with most of the crisps and sandwiches being either eaten or dropped and then kicked around the room before becoming crushed into the very cracks between the floorboards.

Highlight of the evening, though, must have been the appearance of Brian's Guest of honour, Ken Bird, who, to the accompaniment of a round of applause, extolled the virtues of cycling, commending the club for its first ten years and how we should all hope for a further ten under Brian's presidency.

As the party neared its natural end, Brian did reveal that it was with a certain amount of pride that he stood there, shuffling and fidgeting, (as is his wont) and with something of a lump in his throat while he pondered the last ten years, and realised that all these people had at one time been a part of his creation – either that or the lump had been caused by swallowing too big a mouthful of sausage roll.

The 'Ten Counties' YH Tour, October 1982

Improving upon the previous season's 'Tour of the Nine Counties', this year a tenth county – Wiltshire – was added to the itinerary in order to take in a whistle-stop at Swindon. (Although in order to arrive at Wiltshire, technically it would be necessary to cycle into Berkshire or Gloucestershire from Oxford, or else via Berkshire if exiting through Buckingham, and thereby making this a tour of 13 counties. However, a digression...)

A party of five completed the tour: Brian, Derek, Martin Baker, Julian Horler and Iain Macknish, with this tour's jetsam being Mark Young (number 379) and Danny Easton (number 381), who, in point of fact, cycled with the party all the way to the Oxford YH – such must have been the club's appeal – and resulted in a quite unscheduled stopover at an already overbooked hostel. Indeed, by comparison to the leaner times only just around the corner, this instalment in the Green Street Green chronicles would come to be seen as very much a part of the club's halcyon days.

Except for a detour by the group into Swindon to visit The Great Western Museum – a one-time chapel of worship but now housing much railwayana, including old steam engines and carriages from the nineteenth century – the towns of Charlecote, near Stratford-upon-Avon, Worcester and Charwelton were also visited – the latter home to part of the Great Central Railway line, though now merely the track bed and sidings well-known for the trucks carrying locally mined ore for distribution throughout the country.

Spotted by both Brian and Derek was an interesting piece of railway infrastructure known as the Catesby Tunnel, which was notorious for flooding but which, nonetheless, interested the pair sufficiently to warrant a return to the area during a later tour – in fact, during the club's swan song tour in 1988 – in which both came prepared with the oversized wellingtons, waterproof and torches they believed necessary to traverse the 3,000 yards of mud, water and total darkness. Now hands up who *cannot* see the cycling connection here?

Back home, and throughout November, it was business as usual, with weekend rides, including some of the old favourites such as Box Hill, Whipps Cross (although this time making it only as far as North Woolwich), Tunbridge Wells and Aylesford, and a new destination to Rat's Castle near Hadlow in Kent, suggested by member number 374 Julian Horler on account of a Brummie girl by the name of Marlene he'd once met there and hoped he might bump into again! The year concluded without a single ride in December, a particularly cold start to the winter of 1982–83.

Now, had it been the minuscule food portions at the previous year's do, the cheap imported beer or else Brian's even cheaper Christmas aftershave that caused the annual Worlds End Lane Christmas and year-end clear-up to attract only eight? Either way, the end-of-year party numbers at Brian's would prove a reasonably faithful indicator of future Club trends.

Introduction to 1983

Although a measurably quieter year than that marking the end of Green Street Green's first decade, 1983 still went on to record several highs which might have suggested the club's active continuation well into the 1990s.

A slightly worrying trend, and one presaging, perhaps, the beginning of the club's decline, was the cancellation of both Easter and summer youth hostel tours due to a lack of support, and all the more disappointing when one considers that these biannual tours had been very much the club flagship outings ever since their introduction back in 1974. It was also disappointing for another reason, since it had been anticipated the club trailer would be put to more or less continual, regular use during future years. Regular club YH touring did resume in 1984, however, but to the tune of sometimes only one per year and with party numbers that could be disappointingly low.

Kent–Surrey YH Tour, August 1983

One tour for 1983 was, in the end, scrambled together by Brian and (185) Phil Turner, in which they planned a series of dates to take in the Kent–Surrey hostels of Goudhurst,

81

Tanners Hatch and Holmbury St Mary.

Despite there being only a party of two, much pleasure was still derived from what could often be hours of single-file cycling at a mile or so apart: a situation quite unlike that in which a group of nine or ten might force a pace, here one could breeze at a more leisurely gait between hostels, thereby making the most of the abundance of time in which to do so.

The stopover at Goudhurst, an old sixteenth-century-fronted medieval building set amongst the Kentish hopfields, produced a pleasant day's cycling around the area famous for the Fremlins brand of beer, and also the local pinetum at Bedgebury Cross, only two miles away. The next port of call was the ever-popular Tanners Hatch, a 'simple' category of hostel, and rated by many perhaps because of its very rusticity and amenities bordering the austere. Both Phil and Brian recall the three-tiered bunk-beds (most hostels would employ a two-tiered arrangement); the gas lighting; the lack of electricity or hot running water (instead one had to wash under a single cold tap outside); the toilets, too, were set at a small but nonetheless potentially bladder-bursting distance away. To be fair, the hostel guide had pointed out the 'next to nature setting', in a clearing of the woods in the Polesden Lacey National Trust area of Dorking. The YHA guide was also quick to add that a compass, torch and boots would prove prerequisites, particularly with regard to finding the hostel outside of daylight hours, and the duo would return emphatically recommending this advice.

There is something to be said for the closeness with nature one may experience on this type of get-away-from-it-all holiday, although a setback not envisaged was the taking over of Phil's bed – sheet sleeping-bag and all – by one of a particularly comatose crowd of German hostellers. In the end he had to make a temporary bed for himself away from the snore-filled dormitory, on a sofa in the downstairs lounge and with little more than a blanket, a couple of handy cardigans and the warden's old dog, enjoyed perhaps the best company yet.

The contrast experienced between Tanners Hatch and the next hostel on the itinerary, the purpose-built site of

Figure 25 The author in pensive mood outside Tanners Hatch Youth Hostel, August 1983 tour

Holmbury St Mary, only a few miles away in the neighbouring Surrey Hills part of Dorking, could not be more stark, perhaps best described as coming in from the freezing cold to a fully centrally heated room. The hostel itself, while also set among several acres of pretty woodland, scored with a vastly different agenda, featuring hot showers, abseiling, archery and wildlife talks (and no doubt all in the same room if requested), though Brian could remember only the luxury of our shopping trip into Dorking to buy, and later peel, our own potatoes, giving the dreaded Smash a rest for one day. It has to be said that I agree with him on this one.

A Promising New Lease of Life: The Green Street Green Recruitment Drive, Summer 1983

Earlier in May, the flagging club night attendance figures saw a welcome boost with the arrival of five new recruits: Richard and Julia Wilson (siblings to Louise), Sara Holliday, Joanna Edwards and the particularly fleeting membership of Jamie Hammond. This sudden surge in membership especially pleased Brian, as by now he'd begun to sense that whenever a trio or quartet of new members arrived at the club out of the blue, its fortunes would invariably change for the better, being dealt fresh impetus by the mixing of new blood. All the more so as the new intake was mainly girls: often they contributed a better overall balance within club affairs, managing to inject more variety and humour into the proceedings and, of course, assisting in the attraction of new male members.

June of 1983, too, saw the recruitment of three further newcomers: Rob Barnes, a chance acquisition during an unlikely sojourn into Eynsford (a short ride held on a Wednesday to see if the new girls, above, would be interested in more regular, longer-distance cycling). For Rob it was love at first bike, and, upon attending the club at Keston the very next evening, he brought along with him newcomer Richard Gardiner, bolstering total club membership to 400.

In his all too brief time at Green Street Green Cycling Club, Rob introduced two further recruits – two more girls from Bullers Wood School in Chislehurst: Jackie Pethers and Karen Brand, escorted by their ladies' racers, both utilising the more recent mixte frame design (employing twin parallel downtubes, as opposed to the more traditional ladies racing arrangement). By happy coincidence, and on the very same night, came the addition of another pair of recruits: Darrick Wood's Mark O'Sullivan and Martin Blackford, introduced by club regular Olly Reed and recent appendage Mark 'Ozzy' Osborn.

It seemed Green Street Green Cycling Club would be in for a long overdue increase in both club night and cycle activity, and this was borne out at least in the interim during the

London-to-Brighton haul of 26 June. Attended by a 16-strong team, the party included old timers Andy Turrell, Derek Taylor, Steve Pennells, Paul Gowing, Gareth Howells and David Rumm, as well as a complement of the new generation fronted by Rob Barnes, Clifton Jones and Michael Franklin.

July saw an outing to the particular East-End favourite of Whipps Cross, the first venture proper for Sara Holliday and Julia Wilson, who were both cursed with punctures to their rear wheels. 'Not the sort of calamity to worry a woman,' Brian observed over the years, there was, nonetheless, an attempt to fix the bikes at the roadside. Perhaps it was Brian's by now well-hackneyed response to 'I think my bike's got a flat tyre' of 'Ah, but it be only flat at the bottom', but the girls never did show up again.

The remainder of the summer saw the club partake of the very last Green Street Green Summer Fête (the Green Street Green Organisations body having moved away from the area in 1984), and a one-off participation in a new school fête engineered by Ramsden Girls School, a fund-raiser that brought about a nett loss for the club.

With no YH tour planned for the half-term, Brian was able to concentrate on raising club funds by renewing a grant application to Bromley borough, which resulted in a cheque for a further £50 for the club to invest in future projects.

The Departure from Keston

Despite the new-found membership during the 1983 summer season and the initially encouraging ride attendance for the period, subsequent club meetings and outings did not look quite so buoyant and, in fact, average gatherings of between two and five for either for a while became the norm. On 1 October Brian arranged for a circular to be sent to all recently active members, in effect imploring each to consider the detrimental effect that low turnouts were having upon club morale.

The letter, which can be seen in Figure 26, was worded as an ultimatum. It told of the loss in revenue from the diminish-

<u>GREEN STREET GREEN CYCLING CLUB</u>

52, World's End Lane,
Green St.Green,
ORPINGTON. BR6 6AG

Farnborough 54414

1st October 1983

Dear

May I put a straight question to you, and hope for a straight answer ?

DO YOU WANT THE CLUB TO CARRY ON ? I ask this for several reasons –

1. Attendance on Thursday evenings continues to be low. For the past two years the subs collected have not met the cost of hiring the hall, and we are. told that the rent is to be increased again this Autumn.

2. Attendance and mileage on club runs is only just over half what it was a year ago

3. There have been no Youth Hostel tours this year. Both the Easter and Summer ones had to be cancelled due to lack of support.

4. Apart from a handful of regulars the support by members for the Green St.Green Fete and the Bromley Carnival was pathetic. These are our two annual fund-raising events, and it is basically the profit from these which keeps the club going for another year. Again the financial results were only just over half of last year's.

NOW, DO YOU WANT THE CLUB TO CARRY ON ?

Until we have a clear answer to this, there will be no further meetings at Keston on Thursdays. However, there will be a meeting on Thursday, 13th October at 7 p.m.at 52, World's End Lane for all those interested in keeping the club going.

If I do not hear from you by then and/or see you at that meeting, I shall assume that you no longer wish to remain a member of the club if and when it re-opens.

Yours sincerely,

Figure 26   Brian's plea note to the club, 1983

ing subs collections and the fact that the weekly rent was shortly to be increased; also that mileage accrued via club runs was at about only half of what it had been for the previous year, and that while the year's YH tour planning had been, at best, disappointing, club support at fund-raising events such as the Green Street Green Summer Fête and Bromley Carnival had also left much to be desired.

Brian mailed the letter to a far wider audience than the mere 'active body' in a fairly brave attempt to unite the Green Street Green membership before things could slide too far. But due to a somewhat miserable response to the letter, and after having enjoyed more than five very good years at the venue, the Club's regular Thursday night meeting-place at Keston was terminated upon the penultimate gathering of 1983, on 8 December.

The Club's New Venue: The Saxon Centre, Orpington

During the Christmas holiday recess, Brian set about the task of locating and acquiring a new Green Street Green club room, a site that would have to be chosen with considerable care in order to satisfy the following requirements. The new venue would have to be:

- of sufficiently high profile (a prominent building, accessible to all)
- proximal to Green Street Green (there would be little gain in moving further afield of Bromley)
- inexpensive on rents and other outgoings
- able to accommodate the club's burgeoning storage requirements

The ideal location was found: a room vacant in the local Saxon Centre, adjacent to the Walnuts leisure complex in Lychgate Road, to the rear of Orpington High Street. In addition to meeting the above criteria, the Saxon Centre proved to be a prime site for other reasons, too.

First, there was no hiring fee, simply a percentage of the weekly subs paid to the building's custodians, the London

Borough of Bromley. At a stroke, this removed the very real concern that the club could lose money – in fact, even in the very worst case scenario, in which absolutely no members turned up, it would actually still be impossible for the club to make a loss.

Second, the room in the Saxon was available for Thursday nights, thereby causing the minimum of disruption during the change-over period with the old site at Keston.

And third, since the Saxon was run by the Bromley Borough Youth Service, it was always possible this might (indirectly) provide a steady flow of potential membership upon which the Green Street Green Cycling Club would be able to build.

On 4 January 1984 the club's belongings were removed from the Scout hut at Keston and into the new hall in

Figure 27 The Saxon Centre, Orpington, the new Club room from 1984

Orpington, which staged the very first club meeting of the year (in which nine attended) on Thursday, 12 January. Figure 27 shows the Saxon Centre at Lychgate Road, Orpington.

Additional Club Personnel to End of 1983

Robert Davis, David Thompson, Nick Adams, Neil Suttle, Chris Wadeson, Steve Garnett, Bill Spreckley, Simon Birkett, Mark Young, Alan Jepson, Nick Smith, Daren Jay, Andrew Ford, Paul Mackley, Adam Hill, David Boulind, Mark Eyers, Shaun Grogan, Richard Nettle, David Parsons, Peter Walkling, Clive Rye, Martin Crocker and Donna Blackford.

10

A New Era for the Club: 1984–87

Introduction to 1984

The move to the Saxon Centre proved a blessing in that it provided the necessary kick-start to attract new membership, although, with it, a gradual shift in club policy.

The years 1984 and 1985 would be better known for YH touring than the regular weekend and evening cycle rides and, while actual club night attendance might occasionally top the 14 or 15 mark, a sizeable proportion of this would be made up of the ephemeral 'youth club fodder' who, while frequently engaged elsewhere in the building, would sometimes drift into the Green Street Green club room to investigate. Many, it would transpire, neither owned a bike to begin with, nor showed very much aspiration towards cycle activity, although notable exceptions during this period included the arrival and subsequent recruitment of Ian Major, via Rob Barnes again, and also Jo-Ann Taylor (Derek's sister) and friend Caroline Townsend.

A Change of Direction

The period up until about Easter 1984 emerged as a particularly uneasy one, with Brian observing the club to be moving not quite in the direction he'd intended. His dilemma was how to recruit and then hang onto the transitory membership, without alienating the core club members, at this time: Derek Taylor and Olly Reed, and Gareth Howells and Rob Barnes.

In the past, the club had always been self-regulating in a way that saw outgoing members replaced by what seemed like an endless repository of willing cyclists, some of whom would go on to stay with the club for several seasons before leaving. Furthermore, admission to Green Street Green had, almost to a member, been by word of mouth.

Despite a shambolic attempt by Brian – enlisting the one-time help of an outside speaker who visited the Saxon club room to extoll the virtues of youth hostelling – the club and ride attendance until June mustered only a steady half-dozen or so, perhaps just the right side of acceptable, before improving during the second half of the year. However, the writing on the wall was there for Brian to note, and he should have begun thinking about taking greater control.

June 1984 saw the club over the bad patch that had recently visited it, with the arrival of a batch of new intake in the 430–450 membership range, fronted by Mark Stonham (Sarah Stonham's brother). This, in turn, heralded the welcome return of regular club rides and good weekly club night attendance. Also, several of those recruited during this period of respite, which included Neil Wilkinson, Derek Gardner, Matthew Marsh, Toby Walter and Tom Palmer, went on to stay with the club for at least a few seasons prior to departure (cf. the 1976–79 generation of intakes, during which individuals would sometimes record a membership spanning up to two or even three years).

During the summer, seven new bodies were recruited and, in July, the club organised, and subsidised out of recent funds, its first proper YH trip since 1982 for East Anglia, spending the whole four nights at Colchester now that the three-night-only rule had been revoked. On that tour were Martin Baker, Mark Stonham, Neil Wilkinson, Toby Walter and Matthew Hanwell. Several favourite destinations of Clacton, Borley and Fingringhoe were revisited, along with new ride destinations Frinton-on-Sea and Colne Valley Railway, as well as evening trips to Rowhedge and Stoke-by-Nayland. Figures 28 and 29 show, respectively, the party setting off on the 'Ten Counties Revisited' tour in October,

Figure 28 Start of 'Ten Counties' tour, Autumn 1984

Figure 29 Toby Walter (with his Raleigh Record) watches as Mark Stowham has the locals eating out of his hand at Flatford Mill, August 1984

and also Mark and Toby on a mini-recruitment drive at Flatford earlier in the year.

The next YH trip, a repeat of the 1982 'Ten Counties' heavyweight, was arranged for late October 1984 and comprised, in addition to Wilkinson, Stonham and Hanwell (surely not *another* firm of accountants in the making?), a line-up including Brian and Derek, Tom Palmer, Michael Harris and Tim Luscombe (Figure 27). Continuing in a transport vein, a ride to Longbridge, home of the present Rover (and former British Leyland/BMC) car production plant at the West Midlands border, was included as a new destination.

Maintaining the Profile

The remainder of the year also began to mark the start of a turnaround for the club. There was better all-round support during fund-raising events, as well as a promising weekly attendance of 13, with a high of 20 sustained throughout December. In addition, a week-long exhibition for the club held in the junior section of Orpington library made use of information from posters and leaflets, as well as a bike procured from Ken Bird Cycles for the occasion, in an effort to draw in new members still. The only minor set-backs during the middle-to-latter parts of the year were a disappointing London-to-Brighton attendance of only four, and a sporadic disruption of club nights due to the occasional closure of the Saxon Centre during some of the school holidays.

Additional Personnel to End of 1984

Andrew Clements, Darren Grogan, Stuart Goff, Stephen Quinn, David Walton, Eddie Williams, Leon Cook, Fred O'Connor, Billy Hawkins, David Drake, Paul Germaine, Jason Tilley, Russell Penhallow, Phillip Hicks and Phillip Pateman, John Bridger, Alex Wadey, Graham Dawe, Tom Kaye and Paul Healey, Paul Dominguez, Sean Collins, Jason Winch, Paul Duke and Paul Marlow.

The 'Calm Before the Storm', 1985

At the beginning of 1985 Green Street Green was in high spirits and looking in decidedly good shape. Not since the mid-1970s had the club enjoyed such a buoyant Thursday night showing; 27 were recorded for the week of 14 March.

The new body of members, a majority already equipped with their own bikes, appeared keen on cycling, providing healthy turnouts for the regular weekend and evening rides to destinations which included: Eynsford, Aylesford, the perennial springtime favourite of Kew Gardens; also Pembury, Chelsham and Forest Way, Whipps Cross, Hampton Court, Brighton, and the revival of one-time regular, Banstead in Surrey. The visit to the Thames Barrier at Woolwich, the recently finished GLC-funded moveable anti-flood barrier designed to protect against exceptionally high tides, was also new. There must be many, too, who will recall the Green Street Green tradition of 'sloe-collecting' (picking damson-like fruits from blackthorn bushes) at strategic points along the route to Cliffe during autumn ... well, surely *somebody* does?

YH Drive, 1985

Two YH tours were arranged for 1985. Arundel, near the Sussex coast, during April, and the Essex hostels of Castle Hedingham and Colchester for the week-long tour during August. Tom Palmer and Michael Harris were the mainstay of both tours, the respective tour parties complemented by Toby Walter, Brian Mobbs and Mark Tappenden, who can be seen in Figure 30 setting out for Arundel from the Worlds End Lane starting-point; and also Pete Mahoney, Paul Bowman and Neil Cowper on the summer tour of East Anglia. Club activities were restricted mainly to cycling, while the East Anglian tour brought about additional rides to Chedingham, Guestingthorpe, Sudbury, Dedham, Walton and also the Essex/Suffolk county border village of Cattewade, in addition to a stretch of the Felixstowe coastline not visited since 1981.

Figure 30 Smoky Loakes and crew, start of Arundel, 1985

And the Band Played Up...

Not since the 1978 tour of East Anglia had the club's reputation been tarnished – we were very nearly evicted from Colchester YH – over a particular bedtime rumpus that involved several members engaging in peanut-throwing and the shifting of tubular bed framework in order to block the doorways to other dormitory users. Other activities for that night included a requisite round or two of knuckles and slaps as well as 'playing with the dormitory lights' – much to the chagrin of a visiting Dutch duo who, by all accounts, had had an especially difficult arrival in England, without the aid of a welcoming party. The repeated pidgin English demand for 'light out' is able to amuse even today.

This time the dormitory antics, allegedly initiated by Paul Bowman, introduced the group to the dubious pastime of 'mooning', a one-off that soon had an irate warden informing Brian of the complaint received from a passing member of the public who'd just happened to be strolling by Castle Lane – the road running directly alongside the hostel building itself. I say *allegedly* Paul Bowman because it had taken the warden rather a while to locate Brian (by which time, of course, the fuss had all but died down), and since the incident was never repeated and Brian had only recently gone on record as saying that 'any publicity for the club would be good publicity', the reader is invited to draw his own conclusions!

Back home now, the club set about fund-raising with renewed vigour, adding among their attractions an auto/bike jumble stall and lucky dip – with real prizes this time – that could be won by pulling on a tag (one of an interwoven tangle of drawstrings) that would secure a prize housed in a container and concealed by a lid of plywood at its top. A respectable £85 was collected at the carnival this year.

Additional Personnel to End of 1985

Warren Delaforce, Mark Lapford, Alan Seare, Michael Pullen, Simon Daniels, Jason West, Karl Patman, Paul Edwards, Simon Mills and Robert Cassidy, Mark Rivett, Barry Grogan, Andrew Thomas and Peter Devaux, Richard Hopkins, Gary Hamp and Simon Williams.

The Downturn, 1986–87

After the honeymoon period experienced by the club in 1985 – during which Green Street Green had once again established itself as a going concern following the folding of the Keston era, the move closer to Orpington and the subsequent hit-and-miss recruitment period in 1984– both 1986 and 1987 would, by comparison, prove a grave disappointment. It isn't really clear what had (or hadn't) happened, only that club attendance once again dropped significantly, along with the inevitable fall in weekly cycle outings. It is sad, however, that all that can really be remembered for 1986 was a rather hasty YH tour of the Sussex coast that took only Brian and number 438, Neil Wilkinson, to Arundel and Beachy Head hostels, along with a few new ride points along the way such as Littlehampton, Hayling Island, Ford and Birling Gap.

Apart from the annual Bromley Carnival fund-raiser at Norman Park (Figure 31), the only other challenge to which

Figure 31 Norman Park Carnival: roller demo, August 1986

the club had had to rise was in locating for the Vicar of St Mary's, the Rev. Paul Miller, a Raleigh racer, converting it first from its drop-handlebar configuration to one employing straight handlebars – exciting stuff!

Figure 32 The heavy snowfalls of 1986-87 had done much to quash hopes of winter cycling activity. Note the bus stop Brian had had erected in his front garden. The bus stop itself, formerly of West Kingsdown, had been uprooted during a club ride and transplanted to Brian's driveway in May 1983

It cannot be disputed that the bad snowfalls of the 1986–87 winter (which only began to thaw completely by the end of March) had had a detrimental effect upon the club's ability to survive, particularly at a time when it was in need of all the support it could muster (Figure 32). Weekend cycle rides, after all, were the club's lifeblood, although during this inclement period many an otherwise active club member must have mentally shelved any plans for forthcoming club involvement. Indeed, a glance at the diary for 1987 indicates an active membership down by 50 per cent on the same period in 1985. Throughout the winter, then, only three rides were recorded, and fairly short ones at that, to Edenbridge, Maidstone and Woldingham, and while the Thursday night attendance was peaking at between only three or four, the rides themselves were being undertaken by only Tanya 'Tanka' Champion and Brian. The spring tour of East Anglia (to Colchester and Castle Hedingham youth hostels) restored some confidence and saw Brian leading a party comprising Tanya and recent recruit Jason Amat, and also Derek Taylor and his brother Alan.

Leaner Times Ahead

During a period of ever-diminishing club night attendance – although long before the desperate nadir that would become a commonplace by 1989 – and with no summer YH tour yet planned, Brian resorted to placing an advert in the *Newsshopper* for new members. It was, however, only a one-off insertion that drew not a single response and, in Brian's estimation, there was little point in trying again. A last-minute YH tour of Arundel did take place for club cohorts, Brian, Andrew Thomas (477) and the summer 1987 President's Cup winner, Tanya Champion, which at the very least helped exercise the collective Green Street Green will to keep the club afloat.

Fund-raising events showed much reduced support, with particularly low numbers attending the annual event at Bromley Carnival. The recent departure, too, of former Green

Street Green mainstays Michael Harris and Tom Palmer, the latter a charismatic youth who had achieved minor cult status within the club (and after whom Brian would retrospectively label the 1984–87 period the 'Tom Palmer days'), along with the complete absence of any rides from September until the end of the year, meant that for possibly the first time in its 15-year history, the Green Street Green Cycling Club was in trouble.

Additional Personnel to End of 1987

Bryan Taylor, Billy Kissack, Paul Evett, Peter Knight, Matthew Norman, Robert Creedon, Ian Buhler, Helena Wither, Ricky Flahey, Darrell Rose, Ian Pemberton, John Carter, Tracy Champion, David Rand and Brian Freeman.

11

The Last Bastions: 1988

The Will to Continue

That the club would now find itself in such a deep hollow – a fast-dwindling membership that seemed neither able to attract new members nor show a preparedness to advertise any further than the occasional poster in an adjacent hall of the Saxon Centre or, indeed, a single-line ad in the local freesheet – ought to have been indicative of the next few years to come, years which would see a gentle descent into mediocrity and beyond, and from which there would be little real recovery.

However, there was yet a further blow to come by way of a change in Brian's work schedule. In January 1988, Brian was moved from Bromley Bus Garage to Bexley, where he would be required to work very much longer hours, including overtime and weekends, a situation that lasted until September of that year. During this time the club remained essentially dormant, with the cancellation of weekend rides and postponement even of one in three Thursday night meetings, which had in any case become very patchy, weighty affairs with few attendees now.

At some stage during the beginning of 1988, both Stewart Pettet (121) and Phil Turner (185), independently of each other, raised with Brian the possibility of reviving the flagging membership and restoring the club to something of its former glory. Phil Turner remembers: '*We talked about the possibility of blanket advertising via the schools and local papers and of*

101

doing whatever we could to create not merely a new member-ship, but [a new membership] that would be willing to stick around. Time and again, though, a major obstacle to this stale-mate would be Brian's reluctance to open the doors to anybody over the age of about fifteen, which had, after all, been one of the main reasons members would leave – they simply outgrew the club.'

On a return ride from Eynsford in May, Turner's only club ride of that year, he and the group spotted and then approached a lone female cyclist riding innocently into Orpington High Street from the adjacent Spur Road. A Swanley lass by the name of Katie Lowe, she was easily per-suaded to attend a club night, though, regrettably, no rides.

The LFCDA Charity Fund-raiser/Summer YH Tour, 1988

Also in May was the club sponsored ride to around 20 differ-ent fire stations to raise money that would be donated to a charity chosen by the LFCDA (London Fire and Civil Defence Authority). From the club, six in all attended the ride, which began and ended at Woolwich Common and took in visits to fire stations at Plumstead, Woodside, New Adding-ton and Forest Hill, Rotherhithe, Sidcup and Eltham.

While key members around this time included the brothers Fabb (Alistair and Douglas, from Ramsden school) and also John Bradshaw and Robert Goss, the summer YH tour event of the year partnered just Brian and old-timer Derek Taylor for a tour around the South Midlands adapted from the original 'ten counties' routes of 1982. Despite the diminishing tour party numbers, Brian insisted on maintaining old club traditions such as ensuring a visit to a line or two of derelict railway track and looking for haunted church buildings, or else continuing the more recent habit (developed by Neil Cowper et al. back in 1985) of buying and eating squares of raw jelly straight from the pack while *en route* to the next hostel. Green Street Green Cycling Club could still be quaint in 1988 if not a lot else!

Last Hope?

Earlier in July a second SOS note went out to all present and many past club members in what was to prove a last-ditch effort to revive membership.

Charlotte Powell, a Chelsfield girl who'd only just recently received a bike by way of an early birthday present, unwittingly answered the call, appearing particularly keen to invest her time in the weekly club rides to Forest Way, Edenbridge and others. For several consecutive outings it was simply Brian and Charlotte who would turn up and, for a while during that time, Brian revealed he felt that if the Green Street Green was to continue running as a club then, if anything, it would surely have been with both himself and Charlotte at the helm.

Additional Personnel to End of 1988

Richard Cane, Stephen Harding, Matthew Buckland, Paul Endacott, Shane Speller and Stuart Adams.

12

The Demise of the Green Street Green Cycling Club: 1989–92

Introduction, 1989

For any number of reasons, it turned out that there were no more rides from September 1988 right through until June 1989, with the signing-up of just Brian and Neil Wilkinson for the annual London-to-Brighton run on 18 June. And with the sale of the trailer in March (Brian having long given up the idea of any further YH ventures), the only other club ride for 1989 had been the leisurely day trip to the Bluebell Railway near Horsted Keynes in Sussex for Brian and Derek. Club attendance was well down now, with Brian spending many an evening in the club room alone (in which he might occasionally ride his bike round and round the room until the very threshold of giddiness), or else chatting idly with the Saxon Centre's caretaker. Ever an optimist, Brian felt there was always a hope that somebody – anybody – might just turn up one night, and the reasons why this situation was allowed to continue will be discussed shortly.

However, 1989 did see a mini-YH trip – albeit nothing to do with the club – a 300-mile sponsored ride, organised by the Diocese of Rochester for the Church Urban Fund, in which Brian cycled from Rochester Cathedral to Whitby Abbey along with a complement of four more cyclists.

1990–92

There is really not much that can be said for the very last chapters that made up 1990 and 1991 except, perhaps, that there were only a handful of rides at most. Of particular note was the London-to-Brighton in June 1990 (again, only two present), and the very last recorded club ride featuring just Brian and number 388, Michael Franklin, to Warlingham (Chelsham) in Surrey on 28 May 1991.

It was largely academic, too, that club attendance night was moved to a Wednesday during 1992, and that Brian even bothered to turn up for, and prepare the room for, many of them himself. And so it came as something of a relief for him when the Bromley Borough Youth Service decided to pull the plug on their use of the Saxon Centre and shut down their operation – to which the Green Street Green Cycling Club had only recently become a peripheral part – on 31 August 1992.

The club was not officially wound up, however, until it was decided that its history should be written, during April and May 1995, and despite the almost painful decline witnessed from *c.* 1987, it would probably be fair to mark Brian's drive home from the Saxon Centre at sometime during August 1992 as the definitive club outing.

A good home for the remaining club property (i.e. apart from that which still gathers dust in Brian's loft) was found whilst on holiday in North Cornwall during April 1995. Samples of club T-shirts and badges, the President's Cup, bike catalogues, *CTC* and *Cycling World* magazines, as well as the £500 worth of club funds that so many over the years had tried to sequester (if we're being honest, now) were donated to the recently established Museum of Historic Cycling at the former Camelford Railway station. Not only does the Green Street Green Cycling Club occupy a well-deserved place in cycling history, however, the funds donated will purchase a WW1 army push bike. The Museum of Historic Cycling is open all year round and from Tuesday to Saturday between 0900 and 1730 hours (Tel: 01840 212811).

Additional Personnel to End of 1992

Paul and Toby Dunn, Lee Heagren, Mark Stephens, Abigail Treen, Paul Prior, Heather and Andrea Murray, James and Tim Brooms, Felix Black, James Christopher, Kordel Smith and John Martain.

Figure 33 Barnstaple recruit: Abigail Treen *c* 1990

Why the Demise? A Potted History

There may be several reasons why Green Street Green Cycling Club ran into problems, and without doubt some of the blame must ultimately rest with Brian himself for the way in which he chose to ignore the signals warning of the decline.

If one were to form an outline summary of the club's patterns of development from its rather incidental beginnings in 1972, it would certainly appear that from a chance Sunday afternoon ride to Dartford Heath, the club had amassed a fluid yet sufficiently cohesive following that was almost capable of running itself; replacing the membership it would inevitably lose; ensuring sufficiently large numbers to indulge in what could be up to three YH tours per year; organising its own internal competitions (amongst which were time-trialling and cyclo-cross, as well as the mileage-based points system that formed the basis of the President's and Newcomer's Cups), and also developing the means of raising funds for future activities and outgoings. But to say that the club was largely autonomous would be to dismiss the input from Brian, which, over the years, had been not insignificant.

By 'autonomous', then, perhaps we really mean that the club had become mature, and serious about its own form of cycling – as any other cycling club would view *itself* as a serious concern. Looking back, I would say that this maturity had most probably come about by c. 1975–78 with the advent of the President's and Newcomer's Cups and the biannual YH touring which would shortly become the norm.

By 1980 Green Street Green Cycling Club had really come of age in terms of active membership (perhaps the largest by now) and through touring to more distant purlieus than could be managed in a single day. Some might look back and judge this heyday to have continued to as far as the end of 1982. It does appear that the club encountered shaky ground during 1983 with the collapse of the two scheduled YH tours for that year, along with the noticeable decline in attendance numbers during the latter part of 1983 and the subsequent move to the Saxon Centre.

The brief respite afforded by the 1984–85 period again reverted to the uncertain straits experienced during the 1983–84 season, from which, it has to be said, the club never really showed a full recovery. And as we have just seen, from this

107

time on, active membership and club night attendance remained poor, and with little word-of-mouth recruiting on a scale that could rival the eras of the mid-to-late 1970s. In studying his responses during this latter period, one could almost be forgiven for wondering if Brian himself had by now begun to lose interest.

The External Factors

So *why* the decline, and why the continuation of a cycling club that would exist in its latter three or so years in little more than name only?

To answer this question we need to study what *could* have been done by Brian to combat the problems during their onset. Whereas cycling may have been a more facile, ready pastime among young people during the early 1970s, can the decline of a cycling club such as the Green Street Green during the late 1980s be put down to such influences as increasingly heavy traffic on our roads and the concerns of any responsible parent for their child's safety? (Remember, it had been rare for any Green Street Green cyclist to be seen wearing protective headgear.) Or the advent of the mountain bike, a robust, 'go-anywhere' design of cycle that would in time become very popular although quite inadequate for use within the confines of a cycling club such as the Green Street Green – could the presence of such a bike, and the use to which it would be put, have poached potential membership from the club? Can we really lay the reasons for declining membership at the door of the 'lazy' video culture which would see more and more teenagers preferring to spend their time and, no doubt, greater pocket money allowances, on the decidedly indoor pursuit of the Nintendo and Sega? There is some evidence, too, to suggest that even the more 'serious' clubman-style cycling outfits have suffered a downward trend in terms of numbers recently recruited.

Perhaps it was a combination of these factors, and also – a belief held by several former Green Street Green members – that the club's active age span had become too limiting. After all, it is a sorry statement that at only seventeen, an otherwise fairly keen former Green Street Green cyclist might find himself already too old to return comfortably to the ranks of a cycling club in which he or she might until recently have felt an integral part. And despite several attempts from various quarters to persuade Brian to widen the club's appeal to older members, little would be done about it, with the average age span remaining at between thirteen and fifteen.

Had it been, perhaps, the club's unwillingness to advertise when confronted with the need to change? Again, never having previously needed to engage in the wholesale recruitment of new members, Green Street Green maybe should have made use of its resources, spending wisely on regular weekly advertising in the local newspapers, and also in the frequent dissemination of leaflets, circulars and posters among the schools and youth club centres in the district. Perhaps to have spotted sufficiently early on the impressive recruiting record of latter-day Green Street Green member number 399, Rob Barnes, and creating for him the post of Recruitment Officer, might have helped. Instead, Brian had chosen to shun this and other opportunities which, had they been employed, might have been successful in resurrecting the club during this time. His reasoning was that he was afraid that an influx of too many new club members might prove difficult to manage and that, if completely honest, he would have preferred a smaller, more manageable posse comprising perhaps no more than 15 or so regulars. Ultimately, any club, group or organisation can be only as robust or determined as its leadership will allow, and in the case of Green Street Green, the club had only ever known one leader, Brian himself. Significant, too, is that Brian should cite his own age as having a bearing on the club's eventual collapse: he had been 39 when the Club was formed back in 1972. By 1988, he was 55 and had an increasingly demanding workload, so it is perhaps unsurprising that his enthusiasm began to wane and give way to lassitude. Certainly it was too late now to take up the idea of introducing mini-demonstrations to club nights: simple routines that would inform the novice how to repair a roadside puncture; how to adjust or replace a set of brake shoes or overhaul his bike's gear mechanism; or to replace a cycle chain without getting one's hands too dirty. Or, indeed, to demonstrate a periodic cycle maintenance schedule and, in turn, detail the reasons for regular attention. It is the author's emphatic opinion that many an ex-club member would have benefited enormously from the acquisition of these and other useful tips throughout their brief cycling career.

Would it have been too much, too, to have appointed a deputy during the club's period of greatest expansion and subsequent golden age – a deputy who would have taken care of the newer members not used to cycling a distance of 60 miles on their debut outing? Included in this group, too, might have been an element wishing to ride no further than 25 miles at a time. In this way, a two-tier system might have been organised, thereby catering for members' differing needs and at the same time providing all the necessary back-up and resources to keep the club running should the main leader, Brian in this instance, ever find himself indisposed.

In Conclusion

So the club had had around 15 good years before membership began to falter, but whatever its status during the final death throes, nobody will ever be able to take away the many enjoyable years of the Green Street Green Cycling Club, a club which, led by local founder Brian Loakes, was, for many, a formative part of their adolescent years*. And is it not telling, too, to observe the way in which the club finally dismembered? Though Brian had watched the Green Street Green reduce to a membership of just one by 1992, it was clear that he would still prefer somebody else to kill it off rather than do the deed himself. And perhaps therein lies the moral: old cycle club leaders don't die, they merely get left behind...

*See the pages of former members' quotes at the end of the Epilogue.

110

Figure 34 Worlds End Tour: founder, Brian Loakes, atop his 1990 Strada Carrera during 1993

EPILOGUE

A Green Street Green Cycling Club MK II?

There has been talk recently of re-forming the club, building from a nucleus of Brian, the author and possibly Derek Taylor and a few other interested parties. However, due to the reality of work commitments, family circumstances and the conflicting routines of all concerned, there would be too many obstacles present to contemplate the serious reformation of a regular club.

It came to light, however, that Susie Litton (GSGCC member number 30), now living in Dorset, had never really lost her appetite for cycling (and, again, perhaps Brian should answer to this), and for quite a while now has been cycling with her own children, Robert and Helen, around the Wimborne area – with definite plans one day to expand this arrangement into a more sizeable following that might embody children from the local schools and perhaps as far as the New Forest region. A keen former Green Street Green cyclist herself, there is every possibility now that the Green Street Green Cycling Club of old could continue to exist through Susie's as yet unnamed offshoot.

Quotes From Former Members

'Whether the ride be a long or a short one, I'd say we had been fairly keen all-weather cyclists: come rain or shine, I recall, Brian always seemed to wear shorts though he never appeared to get cold or tired ... equipped only with our bikes and a sandwich each, it seemed not to matter whether we were going just to Dartford Heath, or to as far afield as Southend-on-Sea – we had not a care in the world.'

and,

'For me, there is little doubt that Green Street Green Cycling Club had been a tremendous influence, providing me with a keen interest in bikes. From Green Street Green, I went on to work at Ken Bird's – later managing his Anerly branch – and, from there, moving into a managerial position at the frame-building plant at the Holdsworth factory in Anerley. I had also worked as a mechanic with the GB team during stage races in Belgium and, of course, I am still racing at a high level today. None of this would have been at all possible without Brian and the Green Street Green Cycling Club and especially considering that before I'd joined the club, I'd been quite happy with my three-speed Raleigh Chopper!' **Mike Thorogood, 043**

'At the time, Green Street Green Cycling Club was the best thing for both Matthew and Joanna. Both had been keen cyclists and, during their time with the cub, had become heavily involved with all aspects of it – particularly Matthew. I felt the fresh air and exercise had been especially good for them.' **Kath Gray (mother of Matthew and Jo Gray, 212 and 238)**

'The main reason for my joining [the club] was a social one, meeting friends on a Thursday night and again during the Sunday rides, after which I'd always felt a sense of achievement – the most memorable ride for me being my first London-to-Brighton ride ... I am still friends with several former members and we still reminisce over times past.' **Angela Hudson (née Daws), 323**

'The club was all about "having a good laugh" and, in fact, many of us would shun the more serious club activities such as time-trialling, in favour of a ride in the woods. I would say the Green Street Green Cycling Club experience afforded many the opportunity to spend a lot of time outdoors; to visit a good few places – some quite far afield; to try youth hostelling and, I suppose, to pick up the odd scar or six; indeed by the time I'd left, I reckon I had achieved a respectable level of fitness ... and, as an illustration of how relaxed the club could be compared with, say, other, more "serious" racing-style clubs in

the area, many a Sunday return journey would be to the accompaniment of a small transistor so that we could catch whatever was left of the top 40!' **Robin Mazinke, 223**

'There can be little doubt of the impact the Green Street Green has had upon my subsequent cycling career – having been introduced to the joys of club hostelling, I have since embarked upon many summers of solo touring often spanning the length and breadth of Britain. Not only that, but I currently race between three and five times a week and recently achieved 30th position in the National 12-hour Championship and will enter the National Hill Climb in October 1995 ... asked whether there could be life after Green Street Green, I would reply by saying that I would be one of the first to want to rejoin the club should there be a reformation, and particularly where YH touring would be concerned. What sticks in my mind most about the club? The coining of the expression: "Brian's Wheel" – i.e. a tyre permanently flat at the bottom!' **Derek Taylor, 335**

'One of the more prominent memories I have of club rides is that it would always appear to be sunny – just as old people will don the rose-tinted specs. and reminisce about the "endless summers" of their youth, so I, too, recall the "endless cycling summers" of my adolescence. You know, even the winters appeared milder than they do these days! ... It's the silly things one remembers, such as the party arriving at Tonbridge and hiring a boat with inevitable consequences: us capsizing the boat and losing our deposits: or the time that Kevin Walford (No. 56) would attempt in earnest to make it to Dartford Heath on a three-speed Raleigh Chopper ... indeed as far as I'm concerned, very little in adult life now can compare with riding down Polhill at some 45 m.p.h. on the wrong side of the road while leaning over the handlebars with your nose a mere six inches from the front wheel – quite how I, and many others from the club, are still alive today, goodness only knows! Truly, they were wonderful days and I will always be grateful to Brian for them.' **Keith Howkins, 055**

114

'Green Street Green Cycling Club would be one of the first social events I would become involved in during my efforts to be independent from my parents and had been suggested to me by some friends at school ... The Thursday night meetings were chaotic and I'm not sure how Brian managed to put up with us – I remember there was always something getting damaged or broken, in fact I'm not surprised the club kept getting banned and had had to move around so much! ... Brian is such a caring man and it is perhaps only now that some of us realise just how much he'd put into organising the club.'
Sarah Stonham, 243

'The club for me, had been a meeting-place for both existing friends and also new ones. Of course, looking back on it, the Cycling Club was an important initial step in becoming independent from my family and at a time when one could easily have become involved in less worthy ventures. From a road safety point of view, too, the club would later prove useful in helping build road sense for when learning to drive and ride motor bikes.' **Fiona Brown (née MacInnis), 268**

'Even the disasters I can laugh at now, like the time at Yalding Weir when I slipped and cut my chin wide open. It was only when small children started to run away in horror and their parents looked on disapprovingly that I realised I had been bleeding profusely and that something was seriously wrong ... also, there were some rides that never seemed to end, such as the one from Hampton Court Palace back to Green Street Green. When asking how much further we had to go, the stock reply would always seem to be "only another five miles" which seemed to be repeated ... every five or so miles! They were all good times, though, and I've often wondered if the club is still going.' **Jeremy Lay, 151**

And last of all, a quote from the Club Founder and President himself, Brian Loakes:

'The club had brought me so much satisfaction over the years, particularly when I recall the YH touring we had done. Now that the club is no more, however, I find I am particularly touched by the fact that I'm still in fairly frequent contact with several former members. Not a Christmas will go by without my receiving a card from many and during the year, too, I can always expect to receive letters and postcards reaffirming, for me, that the club must also have meant something to them.'

Brown – MacInnis

Gary Brown from Bromley and Fiona MacInnis from Bromley were married at St John the Baptist, West Wickham on June 6.

The bride was attended by Sarah Stonham, Nicole De Saran and Jamaine Woodward. The best man was Neil Donaldson.

BROWN – LITTON

Mr Philip John Brown, only son of the late Mr and Mrs R. Brown, of Orpington, and Miss Susan Caroline Litton, only daughter of Mr and Mrs A. Litton, of Tile Farm Road, Orpington, were married at St Giles' Church, Farnborough on July 18.
The bride was attended by Catherine Forsyth and Mr Tex Crampin was best man.

Figure 35 Wedding photos of former club members Litton and MacInnis – now both Brown!

APPENDIX I: A LISTING OF REGULAR CLUB OUTINGS AND YH TOURS

CLUB OUTINGS 1972–1991

(Figure in brackets ( ) denotes total number of times visited)

ADDINGTON, Surrey (2)
ALL HALLOWS, Isle of Grain (2)
ARDINGLY, Sussex (3)
ASHDOWN FOREST (2)
AYLESFORD, near Maidstone (14)

BANSTEAD, Surrey (2)
BARKING, Essex (1)
BATTERSEA PARK, SW11 (1)
BEWL BRIDGE RESERVOIR,
  Kent (5)
BIGGIN HILL, Kent (6)
BLUEBELL RAILWAY, Sussex (4)
BOUGH BEACH, Four Elms (2)
BOX HILL, Surrey Hills (21)
BRASTED, near Westerham (2)
BRIGHTON, Sussex (13)
BROCKWELL PARK,
  Lambeth (2)
BUCKLAND, near Reigate (1)

CATERHAM, Surrey (3)
CHARTWELL, Westerham (1)
CHELSHAM/WARLINGHAM,
  Surrey (5)
CHEVENING, near Brasted (1)
CHIDDINGSTONE,
  Edenbridge (6)
CHIPSTEAD, Sevenoaks (3)
CHISLEHURST, Kent (2)
CLIFFE, Isle of Grain (8)

COBHAM, Rochester Way (2)
CROYDON, Surrey (1)
CRYSTAL PALACE, SE26 (5)
CUXTON, Medway (1)

DANSON PARK, Welling (1)
DARTFORD HEATH,
  Dartford (39)
DORKING, Surrey (4)
DOWNE, near Biggin Hill (1)

EARLSWOOD LAKES, near
  Redhill (7)
EDENBRIDGE, Kent (28)
EYNSFORD, Kent (30)

FARNINGHAM, near Brands
  Hatch (1)
FOREST WAY,
  Ashdown Forest (4)

GATWICK AIRPORT, Sussex (16)
GRAVESEND, Kent (20)
GRAYS, Essex (3)
GREENWICH, SE10 (2)

HAMPTON COURT,
  Kingston (16)
HANNINGFIELD, Essex (2)
HASTINGS, Sussex (1)
HAXTED, near Edenbridge (1)

HERNE HILL, SE24 (1)
HEVER, Kent (3)
HOLLY HILL, Dowde (1)
HORTON KIRBY, near
 Dartford (4)

IDE HILL, North Downs (2)
IGHTHAM, near Borough Green (1)
ISLE OF DOGS, E14 (2)

KESTON LAKES, Bromley (2)
KEW GARDENS, Richmond (9)
KINGSWOOD, Surrey (1)
KNOCKHOLT, near Sevenoaks (6)
KNOLE PARK, Sevenoaks (13)

LARKFIELD, near Maidstone (1)
LEIGH, near Tonbridge (11)
LESSNESS ABBEY, Belvedere (2)
LEYTONSTONE, E11 (1)
LIMPSFIELD, near Oxted (1)
LONGFIELD, Kent (3)
LONG REACH, Dartford
 Marshes (11)
LULLINGSTONE VILLA,
 Swanley (1)

MAIDSTONE, Kent (15)
MARSH GREEN, near
 Edenbridge (1)
MEOPHAM, Kent (1)
MEREWORTH, near Hadlow (2)
MOTTINGHAM, SE9 (1)

NORTH WOOLWICH, near
 Silvertown (2)

OTFORD, Kent (3)
OUTWOOD, near Redhill (1)

PADDOCK WOOD, Kent (3)
PEMBURY, Kent (6)
PENSHURST PLACE, Kent (2)
POLHILL, Badgers Mount,
 Kent (1)

RAT'S CASTLE, near Hadlow,
 Kent (1)
REIGATE, Surrey (3)
ROCHESTER, Medway (8)
ROMNEY STREET, near
 Eynsford (1)

SEVENOAKS, Kent (2)
SHIRLEY HILLS, Surrey (2)
SHOREHAM, Sevenoaks (2)
SISSINGHURST, Kent (2)
SOUTHEND-ON-SEA, Essex (20)
SOUTHFLEET, near Gravesend (1)
SYON PARK, Isleworth (1)

TATSFIELD, Biggin Hill (1)
THAMES BARRIER, Charlton,
 SE7 (2)
TONBRIDGE, Kent (22)
TOYS HILL, North Downs (1)
TUNBRIDGE WELLS, Kent (24)
TWITTON, near Otford (1)

UPNOR CASTLE, Chatham (20)

VIGO VILLAGE, near
 Meopham (1)

WANSTEAD, E11 (1)
WATERINGBURY, Medway (2)
WESTERHAM, Kent (7)
WEST KINGSDOWN, near Brands
 Hatch (4)
WHIPPS CROSS, Waltham Forest,
 E10 (34)
WOLDINGHAM, Surrey (21)
WOOLWICH, SE18 (1)
WROTHAM HEATH (1)
WYCH CROSS, Ashdown
 Forest (1)

YALDING, Medway (26)

*Sponsored ride to SE London Fire
Stations (1)

Club Youth Hostel Tours: 1974–1988

Devon/Cornwall (1): 1980
East Anglia (8): 1975, 1977, 1978, 1979, 1981, 1984, 1985,
  1987
Kent (3): 1978, 1979, 1980
Kent Coast (1): 1978
Kent/Surrey (2): 1979, 1983
Kent/Sussex (1): 1979
Sussex Coast (Arundel) (6): 1980, 1981, 1982, 1985, 1986,
  1987
Badby, Northants/Warwick (1): 1974,
South Midlands (4): 1981, 1982, 1984, 1988
Sussex Coast (6): 1975, 1976 (twice), 1977, 1978, 1979

President's Cup Winners: Spring 1975* – Summer 1988

Season		Winner	(No.)
Spring	1975	Mike Thorogood	(043)
Summer	1975	Steve Grant	(059)
Autumn	1975	Mike Thorogood	(043)
Winter	1976	Robert O'Dwyer	(085)
Spring	1976	Robert O'Dwyer	(085)
Summer	1976	Stewart Pettet	(121)
Winter	1977	Martin McAuley	(134)
Summer	1977	Philip Turner	(185)
Winter	1978	Jeremy Gurton	(183)
Summer	1978	Tim Cross	(194)
Winter	1979	Matthew Gray	(212)
Summer	1979	Matthew Gray	(212)
Winter	1980	Matthew Gray	(212)
Summer	1980	Robin Mazinke	(223)
Winter	1981	Oliver Reed	(308)
Summer	1981	Oliver Reed	(308)
Winter	1982	Oliver Reed	(308)
Summer	1982	Derek Taylor	(335)
Winter	1983	Derek Taylor	(335)
Summer	1983	Derek Taylor	(335)
Winter	1984	Derek Taylor	(335)
Summer	1984	Mark Stonham	(433)
Winter	1985	Michael Harris	(444)
Summer	1985	Tom Palmer	(443)
Winter	1986	Adrian Jones	(480)
Summer	1986	Neil Wilkinson	(438)
Winter	1987	Paul Bowman	(468)
Summer	1987	Tanya Champion	(497)
Summer	1988	Derek Taylor	(335)

(No President's Cup awards after the summer 1988 season.)

*Whilst it was mentioned in Chapter 4 that the President's Cup had been officially introduced as a biannual incentive from 1976, it should also be noted that the trophy had been awarded on an experimental basis from as early as the spring of 1975, beginning quarterly, as verified in the table listings above.

Newcomer's Cup Winners: 1977–1983

Season		Winner	(No.)
Winter	1977	Adam Winter	(176)
Summer	1977	Iain Furness	(198)
Winter	1978	Matthew Gray	(212)
Summer	1978	Andrew Bunce	(240)
Winter	1979	Richard Stone	(266)
Summer	1979	Andy Turrell	(271)
Winter	1980	Johnathan Scully	(303)
Summer	1980	Angela Daws	(323)
Winter	1981	David Rumm	(334)
Summer	1981	Michael Jones	(345)
Winter	1982	Martin Baker	(370)
Summer	1982	Iain Macknish	(375)
Winter	1983	Michael Franklin	(388)
Summer	1983	Rob Barnes	(399)
Winter	1984	Tom Palmer	(443)

From 1984, the Newcomer's Cup was modified to up to 60p's worth of canteen goods – such incentive!

APPENDIX II: A GLOSSARY OF POPULAR LOAKESISMS

Every Cyclist's Essential Roadside Guide to Club Ride Survival

Who could forget the litany of corruptions of everyday nouns, placenames, verbs and adjectives coined and used by Brian during each and every ride spanning the period of his presidency? Simply asking Brian the time, for a pen or pencil, or indeed whether he knew if the shop at which we would shortly stop might sell milk, could frequently turn into a nightmare for those not so well-versed in Loakesspeak. Some even swore that the very means for finding the way home during a ride could often stand or fall by one's intimate comprehension of the dotty doter's dictums. It should also be noted that several of the Loakesisms below have since fallen into colloquial use via concerted effort on the part of a few keen former Green Street Green members – could not this alone account for the trend towards rising unemployment in the South-east?

Finally, though originating from a nucleus of just three or four, the list of Loakesisms below saw extensive addition over the club's 20-year run. Can you spot those relevant to your era?

Loakesism	Translation
ahwhickthrum (sic)/ahwheethrium	thingumajig, wotsit; also used as a greeting or conversation opener
banana skin junction	popular stopping point on Piggy's (see Piggy's)
beink	blanket
bin	hospital
biscuit tin	any Ford model car

bits (pl. only)	children
blood wagon	ambulance
body (pl. bodies)	cyclist, club member(s)
bomb tatties	baked potatoes
coopy	chicken
coopydrop	egg
cornflacious flake(s)	cornflake(s)
doy-yoyo	helter skelter
eating irons	cutlery
Fido	successor to Micky, a red and blue five-door Metro variant
fuff	(woolly) jumper, pullover
gushing	raining
gushing good	raining hard
licket bandy	elastic band (*sing.*)
lickets bandy/licket bandies	elastic bands (*pl.*)
Micky	Brian/s brand new 'A' registered opaline green Austin Metro, named after Michael Marsh, a salesman at the Oxford Austin dealership
moo juice	milk
neddy	calculator or computer
ocken	socks
ol' Chockit	an old brown Austin 1100 that Brian had once tried to pass off as four-wheeled transportation
oofer	dog
ooffy	cushion
ootzus	radio
Paddy Murphy shop	bakery
Piggy's (Way)	Pilgrim's Way (ride)
placky bag	plastic (carrier) bag
Plastic Farm	popular stopping point on Piggy's
puffer	train
quacker(s)	duck(s)

Rover	The current model in Brian's long line of Metro ownership, a 1993 registration so named to suit the 1990 Austin-Rover company name change
(to) scrape one's face	(to) shave
schoppings	provisions, food
snarks	bicycle stretch grips
squashage	remnant of any flattened insect, bird or rodent
squashy 'nana	banana
string tangler	hairdresser
swasages	sausages
Taffyland	Wales
tea shovel (or tickling stick)	teaspoon
thoroughly bad	Mike Thorogood
tick	cyclometer (odometer)
totty shop	toilet/WC
tribe	party or group of people sharing a common interest, e.g. cyclists, family members etc.
vomiting place	a suitable place to be sick
Wreckage	Brian's 1968 Austin 1100, registration RKJ 439G
writing rod	pen or pencil

(Dedicated to Keith Howkins, GSGCC member number 55 and erstwhile specialist in the art of Loakesspeak.)

BIBLIOGRAPHY

Price, Harry, *The Most Haunted House in England*, Longmans & Co. (London) 1940.